A NUN ON THE BUS

A NUN ON THE BUS

How All of Us Can Create Hope, Change, and Community

SISTER SIMONE CAMPBELL, SSS

with **DAVID GIBSON**

HarperOne
An Imprint of HarperCollinsPublishers

HarperOne

HarperCollins books may be purchased for educational, business, or sales promotional use. For information please e-mail the Special Markets Department at SPsales@harpercollins.com.

HarperCollins website: http://www.harpercollins.com

HarperCollins®, 📖®, and HarperOne™ are trademarks of HarperCollins Publishers.

FIRST EDITION

Library of Congress Cataloging-in-Publication Data
Campbell, Simone.
    A nun on the bus : how all of us can create hope, change, and community / Sister Simone Campbell, with David Gibson.
        pages cm
    ISBN 978–0–06–227354–3
        1. Campbell, Simone. 2. Sisters of Social Service-Biography.
3. Nuns—United States—Biography. 4. Social service—Religious aspects—Catholic Church. 5. Christianity and justice—Catholic Church.
    6. Faith-based human services—United States. I. Title.
BX4705.C2458875A3   2014
282'.73090512—dc23

14 15 16 17   RRD(H)   10 9 8 7 6 5 4 3 2 1

In gratitude to our "foremothers" who have made this flowering
of opportunity possible: 250+ years of women religious
(nuns and sisters) in the United States,
and more specifically all the people (board, staff, members)
who have made NETWORK what it is today.

CONTENTS

⌐

PREFACE

~

"Come, Holy Spirit!"

No one remembers who first said, "Road trip." But it was immediately clear that going on the road was the way to use our moment of notoriety. I had a map in my head, and I knew we were going on a bus. I knew that it was going to be a "wrapped bus," because someone said that's what you do with these sorts of tours. I didn't know what a wrapped bus was. I was thinking big yellow school bus, of course. That's the way we sisters travel. Turns out that a wrapped bus is basically a huge wheeled billboard—a bus was plastered in these amazing vinyl decals and presto! There was our message, and our mission, in big letters and bright colors for everyone to see.

That visibility was the whole idea, but we sisters were so new to this game that we still found it all so stunning and wonderful—for the most part. We were planning a twenty-seven-hundred-mile trip across nine states in two weeks to highlight the ongoing suffering of our working poor and middle-class people, struggling to claw and scrape their way out of the stagnant economy.

When the bus rental company personnel told us that we would need a campaign-style bus with just twelve seats plus a bathroom, kitchen area, lounge seating, and storage, we protested.

"But we're nuns. We're not used to such luxury," I told them.

"Trust us, you're going to be on the bus a long time. You'll need it," they said. "But if you want, we can make the outside look trashy."

Well, we didn't want trashy. But we did need a name. We needed something to push back against our critics and put out a positive message amid the rancor—to show everyone just what we were doing, and who we were doing it for.

NETWORK was founded in 1972 by forty-seven Catholic sisters on a shoestring budget. They opened a two-person Washington office to lobby for federal policies and legislation that promote economic and social justice, and NETWORK has been pursuing that mission ever since. I was hired as NETWORK's executive director in 2004, in the midst of the Bush era. By 2012, although President Obama had brought many changes to Washington, the ascendancy of tea party Republicans in the 2010 midterm elections was thwarting efforts to strengthen or even maintain the safety net for poor and working-class Americans just when they needed it most. And proposals to cut taxes for wealthier Americans was only going to worsen an income gap that was close to becoming an unbridgeable chasm.

In April of 2012 at NETWORK, we were marking our fortieth anniversary, and the nagging question at our celebration was a big one: How do we get our message out? How do we let people know that we are doing this work and have been doing it for four decades? That is always a challenge for a small organization like ours, toiling in the trenches on Capitol Hill. But it is also the challenge for those who know that the Gospel has social consequences that must be lived. Our witness, our only media campaign, if you will, is to try to embody this Gospel message vibrantly and with the conviction of apostles fired by the flames of Pentecost.

At that fortieth anniversary party, we could look back with satisfaction at some tremendous gains that came despite fierce resistance. Chief among them was the passage of the health-care reform act two years earlier, in 2010. But now it was the spring of 2012, and we were in the midst of the presidential campaign. The poor and working poor and even the middle class—what was left of it—were thwarted at every turn by an inequitable system that was rigged against them. At the same time, a polarized and paralyzed Washington establishment seemed more interested in scoring political points than in addressing the real needs, the true cry of the people. It was appalling!

So how could we let people know about our organization? How would we get our message out? We came up with a couple small ideas as we brainstormed at the anniversary party: take out a Google ad (because we could not afford a print ad), ask a current NETWORK member to sign up a new member, that sort of thing. Nothing game-changing, as they say in Washington.

But just four days after our celebration, on April 18, 2012, the Vatican answered our question for us: Rome announced, to everyone's surprise, that it was censuring the umbrella group for the leadership of most of the Catholic sisters in the United States, more than fifty thousand of us, because, Vatican leaders said, we promoted "radical feminist themes"—whatever those are. Also, we were supposedly guilty of focusing on social justice concerns at the expense of opposing abortion and gay marriage and other doctrinal priorities for the hierarchy. They even named our little organization as a source of the problem. Well, yes, social justice is what Catholic sisters do. It is what the women religeous[1] have done for centuries. It is who we are, especially here in the United States. And it is specifically what NETWORK was founded for, which is apparently the reason the Vatican edict singled us out for a special mention. As if feeding the hungry, clothing the naked, and housing the homeless was not orthodox.

As the sages warn, "Be careful for what you pray for!" We wanted to let people know we existed and what we were doing, and we certainly got our wish—though by a route we never expected. American Catholics, and the public generally, reacted to the Vatican censure by expressing heartfelt support for the sisters at every turn. That seems to have surprised the Church's leadership in Rome. But we had the job of turning this opportunity into a moment for mission. So a month later, on May 14, 2012, we had a planning meeting in our office with a wide range of our colleagues in like-minded secular organizations to try to figure out what exactly to do. There was only one ground rule: this was not about changing the Catholic Church; this was about advancing our mission for economic justice.

Little over an hour later, we knew we were going on the road, and that we were going to be in a wrapped bus. And we were going speak out against the draconian Republican budget championed by Wisconsin congressman Paul Ryan, and we were going to lift up the work of our sisters. What we found so frustrating in Representative Ryan's proposals was that Catholic sisters so often used and leveraged government funds to create highly effective and accountable social programs. No one was telling that story, or pointing out that these were the very programs that would be devastated by the Ryan budget. That's the reality that we wanted to communicate, and in the process we wanted to remind our people about the American story of community and solidarity that once defined our society's ideals.

Squeezed between the Vatican on one side and Capitol Hill on the other, we felt that hitting the road became a no-brainer. We could argue all day or we could go out to the people whose genuine suffering we wanted to make known so that we the people could recognize their plight and together find solutions for the common good.

E-mails flew back and forth over how to brand the bus, and after much debate I chose what I thought was a straightforward title, and nicely descriptive: "Nuns drive for faith, family, and fairness."

We liked the phrase "Nuns drive" because we didn't want something passive, and we didn't want people talking about "Nuns on the Run," because that might connote that we were running away. "Nuns drive!" That was strong and indicated a forward-thinking message that we aim to deliver.

So we gave that to our designer to come up with a logo. But she thought it was the tagline, not the headline. Around the NET-WORK office we had been referring to the trip among ourselves as the "Nuns on the Bus" tour, a kind of cheeky, in-house reference that was obviously too frivolous to use for the actual event.

Or not. When our communications team passed my longer slogan to our designer, Gene Kim, she assumed the real name was still "Nuns on the Bus." And that's what came back: a beautiful logo that read: "Nuns on the Bus: A drive for faith, family, and fairness."

We knew right away that it was perfect. The Holy Spirit was at work again, and "Nuns on the Bus" was born.

Over the next weeks and months, Nuns on the Bus went viral—a rolling phenomenon that caught the public's imagination and reflected the anxious mood in our nation, our citizens' sense that something fundamental was wrong and some fundamental change was needed to set things aright.

The people we met, the stories they told us, were the fuel that drove us onward.

Their stories, those people, were what I brought with me that September when, still more improbably, I found myself on center stage and in a prime-time speaking slot at the Democratic National Convention. I was given six precious minutes to present our case—our mission—on behalf of a responsible nation that cares for the 100 percent and refuses to let anyone be lost and forgotten in a society as affluent as ours. "I am my sister's keeper! I am my brother's keeper!" I told the rapt crowd and a huge global audience watching on television and via the Internet.

It is a cry that has resonated from the pages of sacred scripture for thousands of years. It is a cry that will echo far into the future. For our brief moment on this earth, we are called to amplify that message, and I have been blessed with a special platform to help in that sacred cause.

"Disbelief" hardly describes how I feel when I look at the path of my life and the eruption of events that have marked my journey in this world over the past couple of years.

The spiritual life has led me to surprising places that are both sacred and awe filled—and at times not a little frightening. At each twist and turn I have been keenly aware—or soon became aware—of the presence of the divine. It has been my long-standing spiritual practice to reflect daily and to try to be aware of what I am being called to, or where I am being led, and what a willing heart should do in response to that call. It isn't easy, but at the heart of the lived experience, as in all of life, that call, and our response, is a sacred gift.

Religious life has been the adventure that Pope Francis speaks of when he says, "Consecrated (Religious) life is prophecy. God asks us to fly the nest and to be sent to the frontiers of the world, avoiding the temptation to 'domesticate' them. This is the most concrete way of imitating the Lord."[2] It is living on the edge of the gospel in life that is so alluring to my spirit.

The Nuns on the Bus phenomenon was such a gift of living on the edge. When I think of the journey we have been on, and the road that lies ahead, I am astounded. How amazing that NET-WORK's small role in working for health-care reform in 2010 could lead to the Vatican naming us, our little organization, as such a bad influence on the American nuns. Who could have thought that trying to use our notoriety for our mission of lifting up the voices of people at the margins of our society would create an explosion of opportunity? I mean, who would have predicted something like the Nuns on the Bus? I didn't.

Needless to say, that all this happened to me, a vowed Catholic sister, is more than a bit astonishing. I can only chalk it up to the work of the Holy Spirit. That's not just a Catholic reflex, or a slogan. I mean it. The core of my being, the most treasured part of my existence, is a contemplative life—a life lived in awareness of the divine. The challenge of maintaining this awareness is to sit openhanded to receive all that comes. It is not possible to hold on to one thought, memory, or idea and continue the contemplative journey. It requires a willingness to live this moment as keenly as possible, always aware of the many dimensions of now. Staying openhanded, treasuring but not grasping, is critical to the contemplative stance.

I also believe that's how we have to think of our economic life together. It's not that everyone needs to take vows of poverty, chastity, and obedience; rather, we all need to be more willing to be open to the new, to giving up some of our stuff, to detachment from things that hold us back—and hold back the development of others.

"Come, Holy Spirit!"

It is my favorite prayer, it is one of the oldest and most traditional Christian invocations, and it is one of the most relevant prayers for our modern age. Today many of us have little faith in our institutions, be they churches or government, and we view ideologies and religions with suspicion. But we sisters trust the Spirit.

"Come, Holy Spirit!"

That is the supplication that starts my day, as I sit on my prayer mat before the makeshift shrine in a corner of my small apartment in southwest Washington. It is the whispered hope that punctuates the rest of my waking and working hours, and the prayer that is on my lips as I close my eyes at night. It is as my community's foundress, Sister Margaret Sclachta, noted that our special devotion to the Holy Spirit is required because we Sisters of Social Service are placed "in exposed fields and sent on unbroken roads, trusted with the problems of today and tomorrow . . . many times there will be no written guidance, every problem being different; therefore, there will be no repetitions and no trenches in which to hide. The sisters must think very much, still more, understand, and mostly sense (the way forward)."[3] "Come Holy Spirit" becomes the anchor of our lives.

It is also the prayer that, in rather grander surroundings, the scarlet-robed cardinals chanted as they processed into the Sistine Chapel in March 2013 to elect a new pope: "Veni, Sancte Spiritus!"

> Come, Holy Spirit, Creator blest,
> and in our souls take up Thy rest;
> come with Thy grace and heavenly aid
> to fill the hearts which Thou hast made.

One day and several ballots later, the pope whom the cardinals chose emerged onto the balcony overlooking St. Peter's Square, and his election indeed seemed like the fruit of the Spirit: his early focus on the poor was such a boost to so many of us who share his gospel vision. He even took the name of Francis of Assisi, the first pope ever to call himself after the saint of the poor.

"How I would like a church that is poor, and for the poor!" this latter-day Francis said within days of his selection.

But just as heartening for me (even if the enthusiasm of our sisters remains tempered by the challenging experience with the Roman hierarchy) were his repeated invocations of the power of the Holy Spirit—a power so fearsome that it can intimidate the greatest believers: "The Holy Spirit upsets us because it moves us, it makes us walk, it pushes the Church forward," Francis said at one of his off-the-cuff homilies at morning Mass a month after his election. We want "to calm down the Holy Spirit," he added. "We want to tame it and this is wrong."

He's right. Amen, says this sister to her brother, the pope.

At the same time, I know that I am so often just like everyone else in my resistance to the Spirit, in my fear of being pushed forward. That's because the Spirit is about change, movement, wind. The Spirit creates change and makes change the only constant. And that is, at times, scary. Throughout my life, as I looked forward into the darkness of the future, I have never known where I was going or where I was being led. Often I have been nervous and insecure about the next step in my life. It has always felt like stepping into the void. But in retrospect, my life seems like a straight line leading from moment to moment. This isn't how it felt in living it but is how it seems in memory.

The success of the Nuns on the Bus showed me once again, after all these years of praying and meditating, asking for the guidance of the Spirit, that trusting the Spirit is the only way forward. I must let the Spirit change me, and we must let the Spirit change us, all of us. It can happen, it must happen. It is happening. It happened when we fired up that bus that hot and humid June morning in Iowa and went on the road.

"It is a miracle." That's my answer anytime I am asked to explain how Nuns on the Bus captured the national moment. And it is a miracle.

But God does not do miracles to show off. Miracles have clear purposes, they are directed toward helping people, toward moving all the people, together, closer to the horizon of justice. Likewise, Jesus shied away from performing any miracles that might be viewed as showy demonstrations, as "magic tricks" aimed at impressing the crowds with his own talents. Every miracle Jesus performed was to help others—to heal, to nourish, to bring others together into a greater understanding of what they could be: he cured the blind man so that he could see what was truly important, he fed the five thousand so that they could continue to stay together and hear the good news, and he even turned water into wine—his first miracle—so that the wedding party wouldn't be spoiled.

Okay, so in the biblical context, the Nuns on the Bus is a minor miracle. But in this time, this moment, it seems to me to be an important one. It points not to the celebrity of the sisters, but rather to the mission of our lives—to the need to bear each other's suffering, to work together for justice, to build up our wider community. And it points also to the Gospel imperative, the human imperative, I would say, to be a voice crying out against society's abuses and on behalf of those who have been silenced.

What I learned on the bus was that there are heroes all over our country, people who struggle so hard to care for their families. These are the heroes and heroines of our time. These are the ones who we want to celebrate, and support. They are the reason I wrote this book.

One evening in August 2012, I was coming back from New York on the train after taping a television show. I was in Amtrak's quiet car when the conductor came by collecting tickets. She recognized me and she said, really loud, in the quiet car: "You are one of the nuns on the bus! You are on my train!" Before we got to Washington she brought me a ticket stub, a little chit, folded up, and asked me to put it in my prayer book. Well, I don't carry a prayer book. I carry a bible. So I put it in my bible, and later I looked at it more closely. It has her name on it, Eileen, and it says that she was the conductor on our train, on that date, and it asks me to pray for her special intentions. So I keep it in my bible as a memory of Eileen, but I also keep it as a memory of all these lives of good men and women who, day in and day out, work and sacrifice and reclaim in our country the truth of who we are—that we are a country based on community not on individualism. We are a country where we live—and die—for one another.

There are so many who give themselves daily for all of us. One of them I always lift up is Margaret Kistler. Margaret died in Cincinnati because she didn't have access to health care. At the age of fifty-six, after she lost her job—and her health coverage—in the recession, she couldn't afford medical insurance, and she certainly couldn't pay for tests and treatment out of pocket. After many years working for her company as a good and loyal employee, she didn't have a way to get screened for cancer—a simple procedure. So she ended up dying of colon cancer. It is precisely because of Margaret's story, and her struggle, that I am working every day for justice and for better policies for our people. In the richest nation on earth, no more Margarets should die because they don't have access to health care. Margaret inspired me with her commitment to justice for herself and for others, and I want to take that spirit and spread that message to every corner of our society. Every corner.

Our country needs to be for the 100 percent. Our Constitution does not say, "We the citizens . . ." It does not say, "We the rich people . . ." It does not say "We the politicians . . ." or "We the ones who got here first . . ." What our Constitution says is that building our nation is about "We the people . . ."

> We the People of the United States, in order to form a more perfect Union, establish Justice, insure domestic Tranquility, provide for the common defence, promote the general Welfare, and secure the Blessings of Liberty to ourselves and our Posterity, do ordain and establish this Constitution for the United States of America . . .

That's how our foundational document begins: "We the people." All of us, together, need to build our nation.

We are a hungry nation, in every sense of the word. Many are hungry for physical nourishment; all of us are hungry for good words, and hungry for the knowledge that we are not alone. We are so hungry for community, to know we have each other's back, to know that we are together in this nation. That's what our nation's history teaches us, that is what our faith teaches us.

In this age of hunger I have come to realize that we Nuns on the Bus—and organizations like NETWORK—are like manna, the bread given to the Israelites so that they could survive in the desert. In many ways our nation is wandering in the wilderness. We do not know where we are going, and often we do not even know where we are. We are spinning around in circles in Washington, that's for sure, and it makes me want to weep. We are a nation of problem solvers, yet we are refusing to engage the most critical questions of our time. We have to solve the problems we are facing together or we will lose our democracy. It is that simple.

Yes, we are manna for each other. And you know the thing about manna? You can't hoard it because if you do, it rots. You can read it in the Bible.[4] So you have to share it every day that it is given. Another thing about manna is that when it is no longer needed, it will disappear. The story of the manna remains, however. For now, there appears a great need for the manna of the bus. It is in this willingness to share that I want to tell you the story.

"Come, Holy Spirit!" Yes, come. And come along with me, for one nun's story, a story that astonishes me as much as anyone.

But come along most of all for what it says about how each of us can be changed, and must be changed. Come along to explore how this change together can transform our society from a dog-eat-dog competition in which only the fittest survive to a genuine community of solidarity and hope. Come along so that together we can feed the people, and thus we the people can form a more perfect union.

"Come, Holy Spirit!"

1

California Catholic

The movies often imagine the classic Catholic family of postwar America as one of those sprawling, rosary-reciting clans living in an urban ethnic enclave with a passel of kids and producing a politician or two, maybe a playwright or a poet, and of course a priest and perhaps a nun.

Well, that wasn't our family. Don't get me wrong, we were close, and we were happy, and we were Catholic. I was named Mary because it was the middle name of my paternal grandmother and because my mother had a real devotion to the Virgin Mary, including a collection of madonnas. But we were a little nuclear family in the true Southern California tradition. Like many of our neighbors, we came from somewhere else—Colorado, in our case—and from the time I was four we lived in a tract house in sunny, suburban Long Beach. Some called it "Iowa by the Sea," because so many midwesterners had come there to work in the growing oil industry, or at the port or in the navy shipyard. It was a sprawling city of about 250,000 in 1950 when I was a child, almost all white European stock. There had been a large Japanese American community before the war, but many of them were shipped off to the internment camps and never returned. Many other ethnicities and nationalities have since transformed Long Beach, which is today one of the most diverse big cities in the United States.

Ours was a one-floor ranch house on a narrow lot, on a street lined with spindly young trees, near the Long Beach airport. For most of my childhood it was just four of us at Thanksgiving: I was the oldest, followed by my sister Katy, a year and a half younger, and my mother and father. When I was eleven, my sister Toni came along, followed by my brother, Jim, two years after that.

My mom and dad moved to Los Angeles from Denver, Colorado, in 1940 so that Dad could go to the Curtiss-Wright school to become an aeronautical engineer. He loved airplanes and my parents were ready for adventure. After graduating, Dad got a job as an aeronautical engineer for the Douglas Aircraft Company. Our extended family was more than a thousand miles away in Denver, where both my parents were born. On both sides, we had had roots from everywhere, and branches that all pointed to the Rocky Mountains.

My dad's grandfather was his favorite. Ramon Solis was born in Spain, left when he was just thirteen years old, and went to Cuba where he learned cigar rolling. He then made his way to New York and on to Colorado where he finally made a fortune in dry climate cigars. I didn't really know what dry cigars were or why they were important, but apparently you could make money off them, and mile-high Denver certainly had a dry climate. "Union made" read the brick-wall billboards of the Solis Cigar Company. You can still find some of those faded murals around the old gold-mining towns of Colorado.

In reality, it seems like he just invented a name for the process and slapped it on the cigars. It worked, until it didn't. Grandpa Solis lost that fortune, got into real estate, and made another fortune, then lost that one, too. That's the way Colorado was in those days—attracting people in search of a new start, maybe a pile of money. In fact, one of Grandpa Solis's acquaintances from those days was a Denver socialite named Margaret Brown, known to her friends as Maggie, and after her death in 1932 as "the Unsinkable Molly Brown." She earned that moniker during the sinking of the *Titanic* in 1912, when she spent precious minutes helping others into lifeboats, and only reluctantly left the doomed luxury liner herself. Even then she grabbed an oar and demanded that the lifeboat return to look for survivors.

That's the kind of people Colorado produced in those days. No wonder we always bugged Dad to tell us Grandpa Solis stories, and no wonder he loved him so much.

Grandpa Solis was our dad's maternal grandfather. Dad's paternal grandfather was Joseph James Campbell, a Canadian who came from a small town along the St. Lawrence Seaway. His son, John James, married one of the Solis girls, Ellen Mary, and they had four children, the oldest one of them my dad. After one of my aunts died many years ago, we found in her things a newspaper article from the wedding of John James Campbell and Ellen Mary Solis. It reported that Ellen Mary's parents did not approve of the match and did not attend the service. Needless to say, it was quite a surprise to us to find out that their generation was doing such adventurous things.

My mom's side came from back east. Her father was Raphael Newman Gwynn, and he was the most "American" of any of my relations, I suppose. He was born in Washington, D.C., on July 4, 1876, the nation's centennial, and he always claimed the holiday was for him. That branch of the family tree had roots in Catholic Maryland; after my mom died, we found a book some genealogically obsessive cousin had written that researched the entire clan, which included a state legislator and great-great-great-grandparents buried in St. Mary's churchyard on Patuxent Highway in 1857.

My maternal grandmother, Catherine Lehman, came from Germany but was part Russian and fled the Old World around the turn of the twentieth century. Arriving in the United States, she worked as a nurse and wound up in the same upstate New York sanatorium where my grandfather was a patient. Raphael Gwynn had been following in the family tradition of becoming a pillar of the community, graduating from Georgetown Law School in 1897 and planning a profitable career when he contracted tuberculosis. They met in the clinic, fell in love, and got married. But he was growing progressively weaker from the effects of the disease, which had settled in his ears and left him deaf. The prognosis was not good, so on the doctor's recommendation they went to the dry air of Colorado to extend his life as long as possible, hoping to eke out at least a few more months of life. He was just twenty-five at the time. He died at seventy-five after raising my mother and playing a vital role in the community.

Grandpa Gwynn used his reprieve in other ways, as well. He ran two weekly newspapers, the *Aurora Democrat* and the *Adams County News*. He did that mainly because he was a sharp-minded East Coast–trained lawyer but also because he was deaf as a post. Yet through the newspapers he formed a sort of political hub in Aurora. My earliest memories as a young girl are helping Grandpa assemble the legal announcements for the county on the dining room table. I was just tall enough, taller than my sister Katy, to help assist with such an awesome responsibility.

Our regular family pilgrimages back to Denver every summer were great adventures, and we so looked forward to being with the relatives. We would all pile into the station wagon for the big drive. Three days it took! We would go out via the southern route, always stopping for dinner at Rod's Steakhouse in Williams, Arizona, just south of the Grand Canyon. Then it was on to Albuquerque and another dinner at La Placita, with the final stop in Denver. Two thousand miles all told, thirty hours on the road. On the way back we'd go the "shorter" route, just twelve hundred miles, via Salt Lake City, maybe with a stopover at one of southern Utah's wonderful national parks.

Religiously, the various tribes of our Colorado clan ran the gamut of Catholic practice. My grandfather Campbell was very religious, almost pious. He was devoted to Mother Cabrini, to a degree that made us sort of nervous and made him a bit more remote to us kids. My grandmother Gwynn, who came from Germany, had been a Lutheran but converted when she and Grandpa married. Still, they weren't what you might call practicing Catholics. They were friends with the local pastor, of course. Grandpa Gwynn was connected with everyone. But they didn't go to church much until the late 1930s when the Ku Klux Klan burned a cross on their front yard. Then they went to church because my grandfather said something to the effect of, "By damn, we aren't going to be intimidated by a bunch of yahoos wearing pillowcases on their heads."

When my grandmother Gwynn died unexpectedly, I was in the second grade. My grandfather took up the rosary and started going to Mass regularly. But he was heartbroken and died less than two years later.

Back home in Long Beach, we Campbells were churchgoing Catholics but pretty average for that time, it seemed to me. We were involved in church and we kids went to Catholic school, though at a different parish from the one where we attended Mass. Our home parish, Our Lady of Refuge, was as new as the tract house suburbs that surrounded it and was just starting to raise money to start a school. My parents helped out—until they had a big fight with the pastor. The pastor thought they hadn't earned enough money on the bazaar they ran. So my folks said we're done with you, shook the dust off their feet. Even when Our Lady of Refuge opened a school, just three blocks from our home when I was in the third grade, my parents kept us at the school attached to St. Bartholomew's parish. At St. Bart's they called us the refugees because we came from Our Lady of Refuge parish.

Of course, we still had to do the sacraments back at Our Lady of Refuge since there was an antipoaching rule in those days that said you had to worship in the parish where you lived. So I went to school at St. Bart's and went to catechism classes on Saturdays at Our Lady of Refuge. I went to Mass, and like many Catholics of that nuclear age I worried about saying my rosary so that Our Lady would prevent World War III. That preoccupation did fade, but through it all, somehow, spirituality always mattered to me deeply, even as a young girl.

I recall so vividly when I made my First Communion at the end of second grade—I felt changed. There was this explosion for me. At the time I didn't fully understand it. I just knew I felt different. It was as if I was just being freed of something. That feeling, that sense, that definition of Eucharist, has never really left me, and I consider that one of the great graces of my life. And at the same time, it wasn't just a spiritual feeling; the experience led me deeper into the Catholic Church as a community—though the community may not always have appreciated me.

In third grade, for example, we had a really bad teacher, Mr. Seymour. He was the only lay teacher in a school full of nuns. Whether that had something to do with it or not, he clearly was not measuring up in my view, and he needed help. And we always helped! So I organized the kids to try to teach him how to teach. I thought that the problem was that Mr. Seymour needed to know how to get all the kids involved. To show him the right path, I wrote two plays, the Thanksgiving play and the Easter play, and we put them on for the school. Everyone was involved (though for the Thanksgiving play it helped if you still had your costume from Halloween), and this was a demonstration to show Mr. Seymour how everyone gets involved. Everyone had a part. That's still central to my belief.

This wasn't a serious protest movement; I didn't do that until the fifth grade, when my friend Lizzy and I organized what we called the Copy Cat Club. The club, which included all the fifth-grade girls, quickly developed a goal of getting our own place in the playground so that we didn't have to play with the bossy sixth graders. And it worked.

It was in seventh grade that I learned I could talk, that I had a voice that I could deploy in front of a gathering of people. I was a good kid, but one day I got called on to give my report about ostriches to the class—and I had totally forgotten all about it. I was sitting in the back of the room, and between there and the blackboard I made it up. I drew diagrams and talked about how ostrich plumes are rooted in the wing, and the size of their eggs. I knew a little bit about the big birds, but I made up most of the information. And it worked.

At St. Bart's we really got a great education, one where faith was always connected to the "now," and that was thanks to the Sisters of the Immaculate Heart of Mary who ran the school.

The sisters at our school certainly weren't those knuckle-rapping caricatures so many Catholics complain about. Our nuns kept us tuned in and turned on to the world around us. They channeled the excitement of the Second Vatican Council (1962–65) that would do so much to reform the Church and affect my own life. And they kept us up to date on the burgeoning civil rights movement closer to home, and the prophetic witness of men like the Reverend Dr. Martin Luther King Jr.

Social justice and the stirrings of the Spirit were part of the Church and of the world in the 1960s; there was no artificial boundary. But the Immaculate Heart sisters' own prophetic wit-

ness wasn't so welcome in local parish churches, or at least not
in the Archdiocese of Los Angeles under the starchy Cardinal
James Francis McIntyre. Cardinal McIntyre was a stubborn man
with an expertise and interest in real estate investment. That
was perfect for the postwar boom in real estate in Los Angeles
County but not so good for shepherding a church through an era
of transformation. The superior of the Immaculate Heart sisters
of Los Angeles, Anita Caspary (whose religious name was Sister
Humiliata), and her sisters were also determined in their view of
the Church and, some might say, just as stubborn as the cardinal.
The Holy Spirit does have a sense of irony.

The Holy Spirit also unleashed a lot of pent-up enthusiasm
with the Second Vatican Council, and the renewal of religious
orders—the communities of sisters, brothers, and priests whose
communal life represents one of the oldest and deepest traditions
in the Church—was one of the main beneficiaries of Pope John
XXIII's inspiration. Yet the renewal of religious life also sparked
one of the fiercest battles in the modern era of the Catholic
Church, one that continues today, as I can personally attest—and
will discuss in a later chapter.

Women religious in the United States were on the cutting edge
of those initial changes, and they often faced stony men like Cardinal McIntyre who wanted to blunt their progress.

When Vatican II called on the sisters to go back to the roots
of our founding charism—as we call the divine spark at the heart
of each order's particular orientations—we took it seriously. Like
the women of the Gospel era, we went into the world to be with
the people, to bring the Good News, and we often cast aside the
extravagant habits—the uniforms—that too often represented a
barrier between us and those we aimed to serve. We were trying
to do what the early followers of Christ did, but men like Cardinal McIntyre confused the forms of our religious life with the essence of our religious life.

Eventually, His Eminence declared that if the Immaculate Heart sisters did not wear their habits, if they did not pray at prescribed times during the day and go to bed at a certain time at night, and if they did not avoid the books he said they should not read, they could no longer teach in the schools of the archdiocese. "It's not like the Immaculate Heart women were doing anything outlandish," as my friend Sister Sandra M. Schneiders, a professor emeritus at the Jesuit School of Theology in Berkeley, told the *New York Times*. "All these changes were taking place without incident in the majority of dioceses around the country. Cardinal McIntyre simply was saying, 'Not in my diocese.' "[5]

It was a long-running battle, of which I caught only distant echoes. Cardinal McIntyre thought Anita Caspary was going to turn convents into boarding houses, and the mother superior thought McIntrye was "stubborn, paternalistic, authoritative, frugal and puritanical." Indeed, he was seen even by his fellow American churchmen as a hopelessly conservative prelate, and at the Second Vatican Council he was considered more Roman than the Romans in opposing change.

It all came to a head at the end of 1969, when the community voted to set up an independent Immaculate Heart Community, a lay-led group. Sister Humiliata led some three hundred women—90 percent of the community—in the largest single exodus of sisters ever in the history of American Catholicism. She taught theology and wrote poetry and died in Los Angeles in 2011 at the age of ninety-five.

The Immaculate Heart Community lives on (I visited them in May 2013 as I was writing this book), and the spirit of independence has flourished in many other like-minded communities, such as the ecumenical Holy Wisdom Monastery in Madison, Wisconsin, which is housed in what used to be a Catholic high school for girls operated by Benedictine nuns. Sadly, the spirit of fear also continues to afflict many of our churchmen as well.

When I visited the Holy Wisdom Monastery in 2013, the local bishop, Robert Morlino, said it was the last straw: he issued an order forbidding his priests from "attendance or participation at all events" sponsored or even endorsed by the Benedictine Women of Madison, as they are known. Bishop Morlino is of course a great backer of Congressman Paul Ryan, whose budget proposals run counter to just about every principle of Catholic social teaching. At NETWORK, our opposition to Ryan's soak-the-poor, feed-the-rich budget was in fact the impetus for the Nuns on the Bus tour.

The irony is that just as Anita Caspary was leading the nuns who had educated me out from under the institutional Catholic Church, I was preparing to take lifelong vows in my religious community.

2

The Quasi Nuns

My path to religious life was more organic than dramatic. The idea of a vocation first came to me in early adolescence under the guise of doing missionary work. You know: Go to the missions! Save the world! My first thought was to go as a missionary doctor, so my plan was to go into the premed program at St. Louis University. I was a great admirer of Dr. Tom Dooley, who worked in Vietnam and Laos in the 1950s and early 1960s before the escalation of the war. His model of hands-on medicine in remote underserved areas fired my teenage imagination.

But in March of 1963, when I was a senior at St. Anthony's High School, my sister Katy, then a sophomore, was diagnosed with Hodgkin's disease, now called Hodgkin's lymphoma. Today it's curable, but back then we were told she had three to five years to live. Katy was fifteen at the time, and she died at age twenty. Her illness altered everything for our family. For me, it brought home the reality that life is truly fragile, and that death was always near. I think that both Katy and I came to know a vulnerability and a consequent urgency about the need to make a difference while we can.

Katy's illness was of course terribly difficult for my parents. I remember when they got the diagnosis, while Katy was still in the hospital. My parents and I sat around the kitchen table after the two younger kids had gone to bed. We sat there talking until late into the night, wrestling with what this meant. For them, the central struggle was whether they should tell Katy how grim the prognosis was. For me, there was no question. I knew that they were grappling with their own reluctance to face the reality, but I thought that Katy would want to know her situation. I made my position clear: if they didn't tell her, I would. In my view, Katy had a right to know and to confront it all in her own way. In the end they decided to tell her, and at least it was all out in the open.

After Katy came home from the hospital, she was able to return to classes, and as we continued to do all we could for her, events also drew our attention back to the struggles for civil rights that was inflaming the wider world. A few weeks after Katy's diagnosis we were transfixed by events in Alabama, where Sheriff Bull Connor turned water cannons on teens—kids like ourselves and even younger—who were marching for their civil rights. During NETWORK's second bus trip, for immigration reform in the summer of 2013, fifty years almost to the day after those searing images from Alabama were broadcast around the world, we sisters visited Kelly Ingram Park, right in front of the Sixteenth Street Baptist Church, which served as the main staging area for the demonstrations in that crucial and awful struggle. While standing there it hit me that those teens had been making their courageous stand only a short time after Katy had faced her own diagnosis. It reminded me again not only of the awareness of death amid life, but also of the call to work for justice while we have breath in our bodies. I remember thinking back in 1963 that if these young people could stand against discrimination, then I could too. I also remember being horrified to think that this was happening in my country, and that so many people of faith thought that it was okay.

I didn't, and the whole confluence of events of that momentous spring helped shape my decision to join my religious community.

In the years that my sister fought with her cancer, we shared a commitment to civil rights. It just seeped into my bones, this sense that I needed to live intensely enough for both of us, to channel her passion as well as mine. As she grew weaker, my commitment only grew stronger. This wasn't a conscious process for me, at the time or since. But it certainly fed what has become my rather enthusiastic approach to life, and to living. Many people often tell me that I should be careful not to burn myself out, but I never heed them. I have always felt that I have the energy and stamina for the long haul, and such cautions have seemed superfluous. I press on, always have.

As a family, economically we were doing okay during this stretch; I'd call us working middle class, in the days when that was a label connoting some kind of security—not like today's stressed middle class. Today, a major illness like Katy's could send a family like ours plunging into bankruptcy. Back then, we just had to tighten our belts and work harder. When my two youngest siblings, Toni and Jim, started in school, my mother returned to teaching, directing a nursery school. It was a bumpy ride at times, as my father got laid off at one point. But they recovered their balance, and when I was a senior in high school, they added on to the house to accommodate the growing kids.

Throughout this period, Katy's illness was a constant source of anguish for everyone, but we coped, and adjusted. Humor is an important gift for any Campbell—maybe it was part of our coping. Katy and all of us used humor and found joy in ordinary life throughout this extraordinary time. We laughed a fair amount at most anything. Teenage drama was moderated by real-life challenges. But joy was an essential part of our household. For example, when Katy wasn't doing well, everyone was giving us holy objects (relics, Lourdes water, Mother Seton prayers). My mom's response was to wonder if she should genuflect when she went by Katy's room. It wasn't a serious question, but more a reflection of humor in the face of pain.

Katy's illness probably shortened the path to my vocation because we couldn't afford for me to go to St. Louis University as I had hoped. I needed some supplemental aid to my scholarship, but my parents couldn't afford that anymore. I did, however, get a larger scholarship to Immaculate Heart College in Los Angeles, run by the same order that taught me in grammar school and high school.

I still started out in a premed program, as a chemistry major. But I quickly got tired of the lab. I wanted to meet people. So in my second semester, I switched to sociology—I couldn't bear to give up calculus, though. That's just how my mind works. And it was during my first semester that I also decided to enter our community, the Sisters of Social Service. (The Sisters of Social Service is classified as a society of apostolic life in canon law and not a religious congregation. Because of that we don't refer to ourselves as an "order" but rather a community.) I'd had a connection with the Sisters of Social Service since I was ten years old. Katy and I went for a week every summer to Camp Mariastella—the camp our community runs in the mountains outside of Los Angeles. It was a magical thing, gathering kids from all across the Los Angeles area, and from across all sorts of boundaries. It was through that camp that I became friends with two girls named Lourdes and Jennifer. I was from a tract house in Long Beach, Jennifer was from tony Bel Air, and Lourdes was a Latina from East L.A. We visited each other during the school year, and it was my first real experience of economic and social difference. But we were buddies, connected in friendship that erased differences that might otherwise have been insurmountable.

The Sisters of Social Service were founded with a mission to be active in the world, a force for justice, and that got them in trouble, but I liked that. Jesus for me has always been about justice, and in those days justice was on everybody's minds, on everyone's lips. We sang about it, we marched about it, and we worked for it. When I got to college, I became more active as well, tutoring in Watts and helping organize sit-ins at the Board of Education.

What I discovered during this time was that I didn't just want to share the goals of justice. I wanted to have a community where I could share the reasons we were doing this. And the Sisters of Social Service seemed like the perfect fit.

The Sisters of Social Service started as a direct result of the Church's own vocation for social justice. This was given its great impetus in the modern era by Pope Leo XIII's landmark encyclical, *Rerum Novarum* (*Of New Things*), addressing "the spirit of revolutionary change" that was transforming societies as a result of the rise of industry and global capitalism. Workers were being exploited, families were suffering, and the Catholic tradition had centuries of teaching, rooted in the Gospel and developed by her greatest saints and theologians, to address these challenges. The Catholic Church's teaching on justice in that sense is not new, but the economic conditions were. Pope Leo's encyclical was the first to formulate a prophetic response to this emerging new world order. Nearly every pope since then has followed in Pope Leo's path, amplifying his teaching in ways that have challenged and changed the world. Think of John Paul II's work with the Solidarity trade union in Poland that helped bring an end to Soviet communism—and that have challenged our cherished assumptions about capitalism, especially here in the United States. From Pope Pius XI in the 1930s, John XXIII and Paul VI in the 1960s, and John Paul II in the 1980s and 1990s, the popes have arguably been the most outspoken and consistent champions of social justice and reform in the world. Even Pope Benedict XVI, formerly Cardinal Joseph Ratzinger, that "watchdog of orthodoxy," as he was known, weighed in with a social justice encyclical, *Caritas in Veritate* (*Charity in Truth*), so powerful that his conservative fans in American Catholicism tried to explain it away as a misguided bit of writing penned by the naive pontiff's underlings. Ignore it, they said.[6] And now we have Pope Francis, who is taking the Church's identification with the poor to a whole new level.

A one-off encyclical you might be able to dismiss. But you can't downplay more than a century of social teaching that is built on the very words of Jesus. This concern for those left behind by the rise of what Pope Francis calls a "savage capitalism" is perhaps the defining mission of the church of the twentieth century, and our new millennium. In the 1920s, a Hungarian nun, Sister Margaret Slachta, saw how important this was.

Inspired by *Rerum Novarum* and the Holy Spirit, Sister Margaret founded the Sisters of Social Service on May 12, 1923, "with the purpose of bringing the old traditional form of religious commitment from the heart of the desert into the center of life and this way to respond to the personal and social needs of our modern world."[7] Sister Margaret had already been a pioneer in the field of social work when she was a member of the Social Mission Society (a precursor community to the Sisters of Social Service). In 1920, as a member of that religious community, she became the first woman elected to the Hungarian Parliament with an agenda directed at advancing workers' rights and legislation to promote the welfare of women, children, and families.

Sister Margaret and her sisters also trained other women for political action, and while the Sisters of Social Service provided charitable services to the poor, the focus was on directing their Benedictine spirituality toward improving society, especially the lot of the working poor. "We are to be pioneers for a better world, working for social reform, not through decrees imposed by power but through renewal of the spirit from within,"[8] as she once said. The sisters founded a school to train social workers, organized and led Christian women's movements, and served on city councils.

During World War II, Sister Margaret led the community's efforts to resist Nazism and to save the lives of persecuted Jews. Another one of the Sisters of Social Service's members, Sister Sàra Schalkhàz, was especially outspoken and active. She worked with the poor and the displaced and started hostels to provide safe housing for working single women. She also used those hostels as hiding places for Jews and others being sought by the Nazis. On December 27, 1944, the Arrow Cross Party (Hungarian Nazi soldiers) looking for Jews surrounded the Working Women's Hostel that Sister Sàra helped run in Budapest. When she arrived on the scene, Sister Sàra immediately introduced herself and said she was in charge of the house. She bargained with them to take her and not the others. In the end, the Nazis took her and just five others to the Danube, stripped them naked and murdered them, tossing their corpses into the river.

Sàra Schalkhàz had an interesting backstory as well. She was very prayerful but also very tough. Her brothers described her as "a tomboy with a strong will and a mind of her own" who would always join the boys in their games of tug of war. She was learned and active in the Hungarian literary world and edited the newspaper of the National Christian Socialist Party of Czechoslovakia. Sàra was engaged to be married but broke it off when she decided to enter the Sisters of Social Service. Once in the community, however, she worked herself so hard—to the point of exhaustion—that her superiors delayed her professing final vows. Finally in

1940, she was ready, and in consultation with her superior she made final vows and an additional commitment to declare herself willing to die during World War II if she might be able to save others. She was beatified at a mass in Budapest on September 17, 2006, the first Hungarian to be beatified who was not an aristocrat. Both Margaret and Sàra are "righteous gentiles" named in the Holocaust museum in Washington and they have trees planted in their honor in Israel.

After the war, Sister Margaret was again elected to the Hungarian Parliament and, along with Cardinal József Mindszenty, resisted the Communist oppression that had replaced fascism. Mindszenty was tortured and imprisoned, and many sisters were jailed. Religious orders were suppressed, forcing the sisters either to go underground or to go into exile. Some entered the Sisters of Social Service community secretly, often without the knowledge of their own families. In 1949, Sister Margaret made the difficult decision to leave Hungary herself and transfer the central government of the community to Buffalo, New York, where she lived and worked until her death in 1974.

The Sisters of Social Service had already been in the United States almost since its founding. In 1926, Sister Frederica Horvath and two other sisters came to Los Angeles and started a community. They barely spoke English, and they barely had enough money to survive. The local bishop at the time started a special auxiliary to help raise money to keep them afloat. Sister Frederica was a fixture on the streets around the cathedral, visiting families and finding food and clothing for the poor—"going about doing good" as Jesus did.

Soon many American-born women joined them, and the community flourished. The sisters started working in parishes and at a local juvenile detention center. They started Stella Maris, a residence for working women, and then Camp Mariastella (where my sister and I would eventually go), and they also had the Holy Spirit

Retreat Center. The community sent its members to university to earn master's and doctoral degrees to become professional counselors and group workers. And the focus was always on advocacy for the poor, the homeless, the battered, and the forgotten—with special attention to the needs of women, children, and families. Communities of SSS sprouted around California, in Sacramento, San Diego, San Francisco, Oakland, Vallejo, and San Rafael, and up the West Coast in Portland. We were community organizers before anybody knew community organizing was such a dangerous thing—or could get you elected president of the United States.[9]

Also, when the Second Vatican Council asked each religious community to go back to its foundation, to rediscover its own charism, the Sisters of Social Service focused on developing a deeper awareness of the role of the Holy Spirit in our lives and in living "out of an informed social consciousness," as we say in the SSS. The Holy Spirit has always been the animating force in my life, as well, and it seemed like a match.

As I started thinking about entering religious life, toying with the idea, really—which is the way most vocations start in my experience—I had written a letter to Sister Frederica, who was still head of the Sisters of Social Service in Los Angeles, telling her about my notion. She wrote back an encouraging note. I still didn't know what to do, however, but I was drawn to the community. I remember that one of the Immaculate Heart sisters who taught me in high school came to visit at college, and I showed her the letter from Sister Frederica. She said to me, "Well, is that what you want?" And all of a sudden it popped out of my mouth: "Yes, it is." My response took even me by surprise. It took someone to ask me the question, to put it to me directly. The way forward was clear, though it had been a slow-cooker journey, from First Communion to that decision and eventually to first vows.

In keeping with the community's practical side, the Sisters of

Social Service didn't wear elaborate black-and-white habits but instead had simple gray dresses—short but dowdy street-length dresses. We were very different from other sisters even before the reforms of Vatican II; that is, we were modern before modern was defined. We were required to drive cars, because we lived in community and went out to work on our own. We were always innovative in finding ways to carry out the mission. When you were received as a novice, you had to have long hair that you then rolled up into a bun. At that time only "loose" European women and harlots wore their buns up on top of the head. We had to wear the bun low on the back of the head. Of course, before I entered the community I got my hair cut as short as possible so that it couldn't even go into a bun for the longest possible time.

In fact, when I told my mom I wanted to enter the Sisters of Social Service, she said, "Aren't those the quasi nuns?" My dad said, "Well, honey, if you think this is best for you, then that's fine."

Since my sister had been diagnosed the year before, in 1963, and was receiving treatment, we hadn't been able to do our usual family trip to Colorado. But Dad wanted to do something special for me before I entered—he was great; he loved surprises—so he surprised me by taking me on a big trip back east, through a triangle fare on National Airlines. We went to Miami and while there he said, "Do you want to go to the Bahamas?" Well, okay . . . So we flew to the Bahamas for a day. And then to New York, which was hosting the 1964 World's Fair. We saw the Pietà, of course, which was on display—the only time Michelangelo's masterpiece has ever left St. Peter's. There was also Disney's famous ride "It's a Small World After All" and General Electric's Great World of Progress and Ford's Magic Skyway people mover. It was all so futuristic, but the future seemed like the present as we took a different mode of transportation to the fair every day—subway, railroad, even a helicopter one day. Dad went all out.

My father loved to travel, and my parents eventually visited all fifty states and every province of Canada. But my mother was the one who had the real wanderlust, and Dad knew it. "You know," he used to say, "when I'm gone, she's going to travel. She's going to go to Europe all the time." And after Dad died in 1984, she did go to Europe, and beyond. Before she died in 2005—on August 15, the Feast of the Assumption of the Blessed Virgin, a date that would have pleased her Marian soul—she had stood on all seven continents, including Antarctica, a feat she accomplished at the age of eighty-seven. That was funny in retrospect because we always had the image in our family of my mother as fragile. From the time I was born, every day when Dad went off to work he'd say, "Now be a good girl and take care of your mother." But my mother was the strongest woman you could imagine. Yet he loved her with this passion that made him treat her like a delicate object and made us kids feel as though we had to take special care of her.

It may have been Dad who needed looking after in many ways. After my sister Katy died in 1968, he couldn't bear to be in the house in Long Beach and my family moved to Orange County. Then Dad got laid off from his aerospace job. My mother was teaching preschoolers at the time, and my parents suddenly realized they didn't have to stay in Southern California anymore. So they moved to Oregon, to Ashland, where they lived for the rest of their lives.

Dad and I got home from our cross-country farewell tour on September 6, 1964, and I joined the community on September 8. The community house was north of Long Beach, in Encino. No big ceremony, no big deal. They just drove up and dropped me off. Five of us from Camp Mariastella were entering at the same time so we met at the bottom of the hill and had our families drive up together. There were fifteen of us in my class. We were a great crowd. Four of the young women I had known before, and most of the rest of us got to be friends quickly. Of the fifteen of us who entered, eight took first vows after three years of orientation, three took final vows six years later. My friend Natalia and I stayed. Natalia died of pancreatic cancer a few years ago so now I'm the last of that Class of '64. The Sisters of Social Service were never that big. Back then we had maybe 135 vowed members in the United States, Mexico, and Taiwan, and today we have about 70 vowed members and maybe 100 associates altogether in those countries and in the Philippines.

One traditional element that we did maintain was that of taking a new name when you were received as a novice into religious life. I had always had a great affection for Saint Peter; I love the story when Jesus calls Peter, amid a storm on the Sea of Galilee, to leap out of the boat, to trust him to keep him safe. And Peter, great and flawed Simon Peter, jumps over the side. In most women's orders at the time, a new novice was assigned the name of a male saint, but we always had feminine names. We were allowed to propose our own names so I tweaked Simon to make it Simone. That's how I've been called ever since, and I am still enthusiastic, like my namesake, still making mistakes, still overextending, and still leaping out of boats—and on some days fully trusting in the call. I pray I always will.

My first assignment after profession was doing parish social work, at Good Shepherd Church in, of all places, Beverly Hills. But it was another enduring lesson for me. Of course the parish was extremely wealthy, but the pastor had asked for one of us to come help out. I did a parish census where I went door-to-door to see if any Catholics lived in the homes. That was how I met some of the domestics who worked in the mansions. The live-in domestics, mainly Latina women, who worked in these estates for movie stars and celebrities, were often isolated and lonely. They had Wednesday afternoons off, and I targeted that time to start a support group for them. We would talk about how they might negotiate for things they needed, such as a better salary or time

off. But it was a two-way process as they also helped me with my
Spanish. I learned that in many ways, the rich and famous were
as much in need of assistance as any of the hired help. So many
of the teens were on drugs—they had everything but were some
of the most spiritually impoverished people I've ever served.
In some ways it was the hardest assignment I've ever had. I was
young and enthusiastic—a puppy really—back then and didn't
know much. But this assignment taught me a lot about people,
and spiritual hunger.

There was one teen who was hooked on drugs and needed
help—he needed attention from his mother and father, most of
all—and he had to tell his parents what was going on. So we set
up a meeting with his parents where he and I could talk to them
together. It was so painful. I remember walking into their living
room to have the meeting. The house was up in the hills above the
Los Angeles basin and had a great view. But very quickly the surrounding beauty was forgotten as I tried to facilitate the meeting
and support the teen as he told his parents of his plight. Yet the
first thing out of his mother's mouth was, "The neighbors don't
know, do they?"

It was through experiences like this that I learned about the
poverty and fears of the wealthy at Good Shepherd. That poverty
is still out there today. In Beverly Hills, they lived in a ghetto as
much as anyone else. Except they had fancy walls. Behind those
walls they were good people. One day I took the teenagers from
our teen group and piled them in the car and drove around to different parts of Los Angeles. I'll never forget how stunned they
were to be in low-income East L.A. and see happy people, people
laughing, playing in the street. They didn't expect that.

Home visits in Beverly Hills could be interesting, too. When
one boy, Desiderio Alberto Arnaz IV—a.k.a. Desi Arnaz Jr.—
wasn't showing up for his high school religious education class
on Monday evenings, I had to do a home visit with his mother,

Lucille Ball. I was concerned about Desi Jr. and I wanted to make sure she knew he wasn't coming, which she didn't. She lived at 1000 Roxbury in this really big fancy house that took up what looked like seventy-five lots. Lucy and Desi had divorced in 1960 and Lucille Ball was a single mom at the time. The elder Desi Arnaz was Catholic, and although she wasn't, Lucy was a really concerned mother, very sweet, very thoughtful. She said she was glad to know he wasn't coming because she was under the impression that he was, and she would speak with him. He came a couple times after that, but that was it. He had a life, he was busy. That's often the way it goes.

I was at Good Shepherd for two years, working out of my office in the rectory every afternoon for about twenty hours a week. The associate pastor, Father Peter O'Reilly, and I got along well but I scared the poor pastor. I described him as "my hummingbird pastor"—he'd run in, blurt out "Hello, Sister!," then run upstairs. The rest of my week was spent studying and in class to finish up my degree in sociology.

Immaculate Heart College was in trouble because of the sisters' growing difficulties with Cardinal McIntyre, so the leadership of my community enrolled those of us going to college in Los Angeles at Mount St. Mary's College to finish our bachelor's degrees. I missed Immaculate Heart very much. Those sisters had educated me from the time I was a child, and at college I had some wonderful experiences, especially with the Young Christian Students (YCS) organization. Sister Corita Kent was one of our advisers, a remarkable spirit and a remarkable talent. Her specialty was silkscreen art, which she helped to popularize during the 1960s and 1970s with messages of love and peace. In fact, she designed the famous "love" stamp for the Post Office in 1985. She had left the order already, in 1968, and moved to Boston where she continued to make great art, including covering the 150-foot-high natural gas tank in the Dorchester neighborhood with what she titled the "Rainbow Swash." It's still there, a landmark.

At first I attended the "downtown Mount," which was a two-year program, so that I could finish up my lower division requirements. We had a terrible teacher for psychology, and I organized a few of us to go to the academic dean to complain. We had better expectations for our classes. When I got back home to our Motherhouse that evening, Sister Rosemary, one of our leaders in the community, was waiting for me. "So what did you *do* today?" she asked. The academic dean had called her suggesting that maybe I'd be happier at the uptown four-year campus. And I was.

The best part of my undergraduate experience there was when I became involved in the model United Nations program—that's where students role-play as diplomats representing a country at the UN to help solve global problems. That was right up my idealistic alley. We even went to New York for a national Model UN program and represented the African county of Mali. We were recognized as one of the top five delegations at the conference.

In the fall of 1969, after completing my B.A. degree, the community sent me to Portland, Oregon, to work as a religious education consultant for the archdiocese. I was twenty-three, and what a great job that was. This was one of the benefits of being assigned to various ministries rather than having to find our own jobs. The leadership of our community saw talents in us that we might not see in ourselves. I doubt that I would have ever aspired to such work at that young age. But I was trusted by our leadership and pushed into the "deep end" of a marvelous experience.

This was right after Vatican II, and there was so much creativity, so much energy. I met fabulous people, many of whom have remained dear friends to this day. I was responsible for religious education for high school and junior high in nonschool settings, training teachers mainly and developing curriculum. I did some volunteer community organizing on the side as well.

At one point, as a volunteer, I was organizing for a tenants' rights push. We took a delegation down to Salem, the state capital, to offer testimony. A state legislator we were lobbying—well, arguing with—asked if I knew about the covenant of something or other that governed these policies. I didn't have a clue. I started to realize at that moment that good intentions weren't always enough to change what needed to be changed. I needed to be better prepared. That led to the realization that I needed to be a trained lawyer if I wanted to continue doing this kind of work, which I was really enjoying.

It was then that the time to take final vows was approaching, but the then head of our community, Sister Rosemary, was asking serious questions about my suitability for membership. You see, I didn't always wear my uniform, and I was, well, direct. So after three years in Portland, I was moved back to Los Angeles so that Sister Rosemary could see for herself whether I was ready for final vows. She decided that we had to meet every week for three months of reflection—and arguing. It was during these challenging meetings that I figured out that Sister Rosemary liked having fights, and not many others would fight with her. But I would. So while this wasn't exactly my preferred way of interacting, in the end we were okay. And she at long last gave me her approval. She was disappointed, though, that I didn't seem too excited about having her okay for final vows. For me, the choice—the commitment—had been made long before, so her approval was sort of anticlimactic.

I was focused at that time on carrying the mission out into the world on behalf of all those people who were struggling. While Sister Rosemary was sizing me up I worked for a couple of years at the Newman Center at Los Angeles City College—an inner-city two-year college campus. There were all these young adults who I

described as "failure oriented." Failure was all they knew in life; it was the only experience they had, the only prospect they could see. I loved them. They needed a success experience, and many of them had never traveled outside of Los Angeles. So we raised money to go to the Grand Canyon as an adventure. I thought it was a wonderful experience at the time, but the important thing is that it seemed to stick with those young people. One of the "kids," Chuck Regan, spotted me on a TV show in August 2012 when the Nuns on the Bus tour was high on the media radar and he wrote me, out of the blue, recalling the impression left by those simple gestures, the dedication to leaving no one behind by pulling together:

> With all the people you have touched over your career, you may not remember the kid from Maine with long hair and beard that ventured into the Newman Center at LACC in 1973, but you, along with Sister Jan, Father Pat and Father Bill [my wonderful colleagues there] made a major impact on me. A YouTube comment you made about our need to include 100% of Americans versus the 99% (or any other fraction) of our citizens reminds me of the 1974 bus trip we made to the Grand Canyon—where none of us kids that hung out at the Newman Center could individually afford to go to the Canyon. So we all went together—through a couple sock hops, car washes and a bake sale. No one was left behind. Keep fighting, Sister Simone! Best regards, Chuck.

No one left behind. That sums it up for me.

With final vows taken and my time in Los Angeles nearing an end, I was finally able to go to law school, as I had first planned while up in Oregon. I needed the legal expertise that being a lawyer could provide, and the Sisters of Social Service were all about

being women active in society—and in politics—for the Gospel.

Yet not everyone in the community in Portland was on board at first. "None of us has ever gone to law school," said Sister Patricia, whom I lived with at the time; she was a few years ahead of me. "So what?" I said. "Well, I don't think that's going to fly," she said. "I think you are going to need to convince people."

So I wrote what amounted to a brief arguing my case. That carried the day, and I was accepted into the law school at the University of California–Davis, near Sacramento, the state capital.

When our sisters went for a degree, they often went east to school and did not live in a community. But I knew that if I was going to do something like law school, I needed to do it in the context of community so that the community grew with me as I grew into this professional role. Fortunately we had a house in Sacramento, and there were a total of five of us. I received financial aid to cover the $666 a year for tuition and I had a work-study grant doing legal research for a professor, as well as volunteering on the law review.

Law school was hard work, but I did pretty well. Every evening at seven o'clock, right after dinner, I would get up and bid everyone good night and go off to study. What surprised me as much as anything is that I discovered I liked practicing law. I'd had no knowledge of this world before; I was a Catholic sister coming from a religious and social service background. What did I know about secured transactions, the hearsay rule, the rule against perpetuities, and third-party beneficiary contracts? But I passed the bar the first time out and was a full-fledged lawyer.

Once I passed the bar, however, I realized that I had been so disciplined for three years that I had lost touch with friends and did not know how to relax, to experience leisure. The discipline of long hours of study had been beneficial for becoming a lawyer, but not for ordinary human existence. The first thing I needed to do was to take a remedial course in socializing after three years

in the law school cloister. My sisters in Oakland were just the help that I needed. They welcomed me and helped me develop other aspects of myself. We would sit around the dinner table and talk for an hour or more most evenings. Two of us participated in interpretive movement every Sunday night. We gathered for prayer every morning and sometimes had Mass at the house when a priest-friend would come over. Although I went to Oakland to work as a lawyer, the time with my sisters there was one of the best community experiences that I have had.

Next up of course was putting into practice what I learned in law school. The research I enjoyed doing most was also—not coincidentally—what interested me most, namely addressing the unmet legal needs of working-poor people. In other words, providing legal advice and counsel for those who could not qualify for free legal services but who did not make enough to be able to afford a private lawyer. The Sisters of Social Service community has always focused on unmet social needs, and in retrospect my work has always hewed closely to that mission. The poorest of the poor need our help desperately—today more than ever—and the wealthy need our prayers and our prophetic challenge. But the working poor so often go overlooked. So often they are the backbone of a community and yet they are taken for granted, or, worse, romanticized through the sepia-tinted lens of nostalgia as some kind of throwback to a better America of blue-collar working stiffs.

Well, I have news for you—that America was tough for working-class folks then, and it may be tougher today. The working poor are just that—they are working and yet they are still barely making it because of our skewed tax system and budget priorities, and because of an unjust health-care system that will still require years of effort to reform. These working-class Americans are one misstep from missing the rent or mortgage payment or skipping medical treatment or tanking their credit rating. The path to middle-class security is blocked by obstacles that were never there before, and "middle-class security" sounds like a mythical beast to many in the middle class. The American dream is a fantasy for a growing segment of the population—the very people my religious community always aims to serve.

So back in 1978, now armed with a law degree and good intentions, I set out to establish the kind of community law center that I designed as a project during my last semester in law school. The center was to serve the unmet legal needs of working-poor families. Using census data, I found that the area with the highest density of working-poor people in California was in Alameda County, and the heart of that population was in the city of Oakland. If the design was going to work anywhere, it would be in Oakland.

I had the design and the commitment of three parishes, and I needed to get the project rolling. But I was anxious, and I literally worried myself sick the very week before actually beginning. I was frightened about being a new attorney and not knowing what I was doing. I was frightened that this idea of mine wouldn't work. I was just frightened about launching out into the deep. I worked myself into such a state that I ended up in the emergency room with my electrolytes out of balance. But nervous though I was, with the support of my sisters, I started this big adventure. After my first day of work, with a full calendar and a waiting list already, I thought maybe I should have picked the second-highest density of working-poor people in our state.

I started building the center's name and clientele by going to parishes in the flatland neighborhoods of the city. These parishes were a focal point for the working-poor people of the county. I started with a summer-long pilot project in three parishes and later added a fourth. If the parish provided space, I would meet with parishioners. For payment, I used a sliding scale, starting at $5 an hour for attorney's fees. Since my idea was unproven, I couldn't secure any foundation grants for badly needed start-up funds. So one of our sisters, Virginia, gave me $100 from the money she had received from her jubilee celebrating twenty-five years in the community. The sisters I lived with urged me to use the community's "telephone closet" for our office. So we installed a separate phone line in the closet of the community's house in Oakland and I got a rotary phone for it, all I could afford. A couple of months later, Sister Marion Donohue, a member of the Sisters of St. Joseph of Carondolet, joined me as a volunteer paralegal. Together we set up the system that would become the backbone of the law center. We continued meeting clients in parishes, and after a year, we had enough money to rent office space downtown in a real law office. It worked, and it continues to operate today, renamed the Law Center for Families.

3

~

Touching the Pain of the World

The Community Law Center was sort of like my child. I spent eighteen years nurturing it, and it was as taxing as it was rewarding—but rewarding above all. Over the years the staff grew to include six attorneys and four or five paralegals and other support personnel. Sister Marion and I were the only sisters there for that whole time. Most of our staff were laywomen and laymen. A few times we had other religious on staff, and it became something of a training ground for seminarians who were studying at the Graduate Theological Union in Berkeley. But my full-time law partners were laywomen who shared my commitment to service for those who are left out too often.

Our caseload also evolved so that we wound up taking most of the high-conflict, low-income family law cases in the county. My background in both social work and law helped us in trying to work with family systems to improve the situation for everyone. When I started practicing law, I chose not to use my title of "Sister." I thought that it would create confusion for clients or opposing parties (to say nothing of opposing attorneys and judges). So on my business card was printed simply: "S. Simone Campbell." Not surprisingly, word got out around the Alameda County Bar that in fact I was a Catholic sister. I remember meeting in the chambers of a judge who was new to the family law bench. He asked me what the "S" stood for. I told him it stood for Sister. He was floored. He said that he thought it might stand for Susan. The important thing is that we served the working poor of our county, and we were highly respected for our legal expertise—whatever the initials on our business cards or the title in front of our names.

Our clients were not typical. One man had suffered a brain trauma that left him a bit at sea and unbalanced. He would lash out verbally and physically. And he was always misplacing my card with my phone number. So his approach to solving this problem was that whenever he felt his anger rising and likely to end with him striking his partner, he would drive around the city really fast until he was stopped by the police. He couldn't remember what else to do. After he'd get picked up, he'd beg the cops to get my phone number. Then we would work out a solution to whatever was his latest crisis. I had to develop certain skills for this sort of work. For example, I represented abuse victims, but I found that I was also good at representing abusers because I would set limits for them. When another big, hulking client of ours was physically intimidating everyone in the room, I just flat-out told him, "Sit down! That's not who you are. Behave yourself!" And he did.

But I mainly represented people caught in all sorts of challenging circumstances, and it was heartbreaking at times.

One of the most challenging family situations arose when I was appointed by the court to represent Kirsten. She was seven years old and had been placed with a family for possible adoption when her biological father showed up and demanded custody. The court placed Kirsten with him and his wife and their two boys and named me as Kirsten's attorney to guard her interests. Her placement was not a good situation. The dad was a recovering alcoholic and drug addict who was not coping well, and the stepmother was an alcoholic too. They were also both so trapped in their self-centered syndromes they had little psychic space to pay attention to Kirsten or the other children. When I went to visit the home, the household just disintegrated in front of me. The stepmom blamed Kirsten for their family problems and the dad just walked out, passive in the face of their dysfunction. I encouraged them to consider family counseling, but the father opted for a different solution: a couple of days later he showed up at our office building. He took the elevator to the fifth floor, where our office was located. The elevator door opened, and he pushed Kirsten out into the hallway. She had a little bag in her hand with what few belongings she had in this world. He made her walk down the long hallway to our office alone while he stepped back into the elevator and left without a word to me or anyone in my office.

He had pinned a note to Kirsten's dress that read: "Here, take her. Quit destroying my family."

She stayed with me for twelve days while we worked out her legal situation. I refused to put Kirsten back in the foster care roulette wheel. She eventually ended up back with her original adoptive family, in Missouri. But if I ever need a reminder that good can come from suffering, I think of Kirsten.

In April 2012, when the Vatican announced it had begun an investigation of the leadership group of American sisters and had accused NETWORK in particular of focusing too much on social justice, I was all over the news to discuss the developments. Marjorie, Kirsten's adoptive mother, heard me on a Canadian Broadcasting Company program, looked up my e-mail at the NETWORK site, and wrote to me:

I don't know if you will remember me. We were attempting
to stay in Kirsten's life . . . We were poor, in Missouri, and
without much hope until you became Kirsten's guardian ad
litem. We credit you with saving Kirsten's sanity, if not her
life. She is now happily married, living in London, England
and expecting a baby this summer. She is almost 33 yrs old.
I just wanted to say Thank you again, and it is wonderful to
hear what you are doing now. Love, Marjorie

Thanks to the Vatican, I was able to receive such wonderful news. And thanks to Kirsten's adoptive parents, her life has
turned out better than even I could have hoped for way back then
in Oakland.

Another powerful example of good emerging from suffering
was a divorce case I worked that was in fact unlike most of the
cases we took. In this instance, I represented the woman, and she
and her husband largely worked together with an eye to caring
for their two daughters. Yet a few months after the divorce became final, my client and her younger daughter were killed in an
automobile accident caused by a drunk truck driver. Her former
husband came to me for help in dealing with the myriad issues
that he was facing in caring for his older surviving daughter, who
had been rescued from the car before it exploded into flames. We
worked together to care for her and to find a way to memorial-
ize her mother and sister. She received a decent settlement out of
the lawsuit brought on her behalf, enough to support her through
what would inevitably be a rough road ahead. We at the Community Law Center received attorney's fees for our work in the
case and in a tribute to our client, we decided to use the money to
create a two-year internship program that trained new attorneys
to do family law from a systems perspective. We named the program after our client, and the Lillian Hansen internship became
a stellar program that helped shape the practice of family law in

Alameda County. It was the best of who we were at the center, and a fitting tribute to my client, her former husband, and their children.

These experiences are nourishing for me because being with real people and dealing with real issues is sacred. They shared their pain with me and by doing so gave me an invaluable gift of hope. I was reading Walter Brueggemann back then—he is one of the greatest Old Testament scholars of the past few decades and above all a wonderful theologian and spiritual writer. My work was about what Brueggemann would call touching the pain of the world. It is living the Gospel, and it is the realization that downtown Oakland is much like Beverly Hills; everyone has their pain, only in different guises. "Jeremiah, faithful to Moses, understood what numb people will never know, that only grievers can experience their experiences and move on," Brueggemann writes. He continues:[10]

> I used to think it curious that, when having to quote scripture on demand, someone would inevitably say, "Jesus wept." It is usually done as a gimmick to avoid having to quote a longer passage. But I now understand the depth of that verse. Jesus knew what we numb ones must always learn again: (a) that weeping must be real because endings are real; and (b) that weeping permits newness. His weeping permits the kingdom to come. Such weeping is a radical criticism, a fearful dismantling because it means the end of all machismo; weeping is something kings rarely do without losing their thrones. Yet the loss of thrones is precisely what is called for in radical criticism.

Working at the Community Law Center was wonderful because we were so connected with people at such profound moments in their lives. Like Jesus in the Gospels, we were with the people who are suffering—churched or unchurched, didn't matter. People want to turn away from pain and poverty and difficulty. Yet that's where life is, and that's how we become aware that we are one body. We attempted to do family law in a way that benefited the whole family—including the opposing side. It was challenging, but it was about working to make the entire family system better.

In some ways the most traumatic experience of my time in Oakland came at 5:04 P.M. on October 17, 1989. Everybody in the Bay Area remembers that time and where they were, because that is when the San Andreas Fault shook and shuddered and then settled, and in doing so unleashed an earthquake that lasted less than twenty seconds but seemed like twenty hours.

When it was over, sixty-three people were dead, forty-two of them in West Oakland (three blocks from where I lived), killed when more than a mile-long stretch of the upper level of the Cypress Street Viaduct of Interstate 880 collapsed onto the lower level and crushed the cars below. Nearly four thousand people were injured, and the third game of the World Series between the Oakland Athletics and the San Francisco Giants was postponed.

Earthquakes have always made me nervous, and it was only later that I realized how much the 1989 experience traumatized me. But at the time, in the moment, I was surprisingly cool in dealing with a client whom I was meeting with in my office. Our office was on the fifth floor of an old building that was not quake-proof, needless to say.

Because we were far enough from the epicenter, the temblor came in two waves, first a big rolling wave and then a big shake. I shoved my client under the desk as the ceiling fell in and bookcases started tumbling. Computer monitors crashed onto the floor, and chunks of marble fell off the exterior walls. If it had gone on much longer, we wouldn't have gotten out. When everything finally stopped moving, I grabbed my client, got one of our paralegals, Angie, out from under the desk, and together with a lawyer, Katie, we headed down the staircase even as it was pulling away from the wall like some crazy postmodern painting.

It was then I discerned the difference between neurotics and psychotics. My client was psychotic. When we got outside, I looked her in the eye and said, "Get your son from school and go home!" She turned to me and said, "But we haven't finished talking about my custody case!" I yelled back that we would deal with her case another time, and then I realized that I was still clutching my pen in my hand, just as I was when I was taking notes moments earlier.

With psychotics, the outside world doesn't enter in. It's us ordinary neurotics who get terrified. The outside world looked plenty grim as we took stock of the destruction. For our law center, the upshot of the earthquake was that we had to find new office space. The place we moved into looked like a brothel at first, though we eventually fixed it up. Our most valuable possession was a copier, which we had to lower down the outside of our old offices with climbing ropes, knocking bits off the eight-story building as it bounced down the side.

Any natural disaster, and especially one of that size and scope, reconfigures the community, and many individual lives. So it was for Oakland, and for the law center, and for me.

The first evidence of what was to come was that domestic violence increased dramatically, as often happens in the wake of such cataclysmic events. I was the court-appointed lawyer in a number of extremely challenging cases, and at the same time I had to deal with FEMA—the Federal Emergency Management Administration—to try to recover some of our losses and costs. Yet the adversity so many of us faced brought me so much closer to friends in the bar as we handled the adversity together. My women's group, which we called the Sewing Circle, became exceptionally close, a critical emotional support network through the struggles.

My law partners at the law center, who were all lay folks and not necessarily Catholic, and my colleagues in the family law and probate bar, were wonderful. There was a lot of salutary laughter as we built a practice that was respected across the state. The chief justice of the California Supreme Court named me to a couple of important committees, and I was able to present my case on behalf of the state's low-income families in a number of venues. I testified in Sacramento about the family law needs of the working poor—the people we served—and we convinced the legislature to change the law so that we could separately incorporate the law center in California as a nonprofit. That allowed us to charge all of our clients fees and provided a vital income stream. We supported ourselves solely on client fees. We took some high-end cases to balance out the low end. The top rate was $175 per hour when I left, and the bottom was $35 per hour. Charging fees was more than viability; it was a lifeline.

My own time at the center, however, seemed to be approaching an end. While the months and years after the 1989 earthquake were fruitful in the end, they were tough, as well, and they took a toll. During one exceptionally challenging stretch, the opposing party in a case was stalking me and I had to be given police protection. It was unsettling, and exhausting, and afterward I took a few months off to decompress.

That's when I came to realize that I needed a change. If the law center was my child, it had grown up in those eighteen years, but it wasn't going off to college. Some of my lay partners had taken maternity leaves in recent years, and I realized I too needed a break of my own to give birth to a new idea, and to get away from the hard cases and the kind of personal threats that were part of the job but that still took a toll. Besides, the center now had six attorneys plus paralegals and staff. The place would be fine, and it was.

Still, leaving the law center, and the spiritual nourishment I had known by working with clients—by touching their pain, and trying to ease it—was hard. It was also necessary. What direction would the Holy Spirit send me in this time? Religious life made the decision for me. I was toying with a few ideas, such as creating a "life tank" that would develop ideas based on lived experiences rather than the standard wonkery of "think tanks" that develop ideas based on what went on inside someone's head or in a research paper.

But several of my sisters asked me to keep my name in the ring for the election of the "general director" of our community, a post that comes open every five years. The Sisters of Social Service is a relatively small order and everyone has to contribute to running the show. To my surprise, I was elected general director at our chapter meeting in June 1995, just after I left the law center. That seemed to answer the question of what God was calling me to next, though it wasn't an easy passage.

In a sense I was walking into the trauma of another earthquake, both physical and spiritual. Five years after the Oakland earthquake, the Northridge earthquake had rocked Los Angeles and seriously damaged our motherhouse there. It was also a metaphorical earthquake for the community because as we looked at rebuilding our motherhouse, we also stepped back to assess ourselves: Who are we? Are we going to survive? Where are we going? Do we deserve a new place? There were a lot of questions, profound questions, that I didn't fully appreciate at the time. But I soon came face-to-face with it all.

At our chapter meeting in 1995 we had this insight that "we are the church, and that we will know it, own it, and act on it." Putting that into practice is tougher than saying it, however, and of course there are all the internal dynamics of a small community to deal with, and I wasn't equipped for it at first. About six months after I had been elected, when I was doing my daily morning meditation, the sound that you make with a straw at the bottom of a soda popped into my mind. That was the sound of my spiritual life. I was running on empty and I had to become connected to other sources of spiritual nourishment. For months I hadn't had a client to represent or a court case to prepare and I needed to find other places to meet God.

Election to leadership of a religious community is always challenging. For me it was tough because for the previous eighteen years I had run the law center, litigated cases, managed clients, written argumentative briefs, and competed to win the best result for my clients and their families. Although these are wonderful legal skills, they don't always translate to religious life culture where we focus on collaboration, discernment, and a much slower, less competitive pace. It was a challenging adjustment for me. It was this adjustment that became the grist of my spiritual life.

Criticism naturally gets directed toward the leader, and in a time of insecurity following the Northridge earthquake and our having to leave our motherhouse of sixty-five years, criticism was intense at times from some members. I also knew that the criticisms that hurt me had some truth in them. So my spiritual meditation practice became sitting with the criticism that hurt me until I knew the truth of it. Once I knew the truth, it released the barb of it and I could grow and not be angry about it. One of the aspects of growth for me was that I learned from the criticism of my writing that I was "too corporate" and not enough of a spiritual leader. From sitting with the pain of this true criticism, I learned to speak to my sisters of my spiritual life. This sort of communication has become an essential component of our work "on the bus" and in our advocacy in Washington. I owe this growth to my sisters and to the challenging time of leadership.

Afterward I came to think of my role in leadership during that time as a crucible: holding the reality of a community in crisis, a container for a purifying fire so the challenging time gets refined into gold. For me that's all the Holy Spirit.

Did things improve on my watch? I think I helped the community. I think my stumblings weren't totally detrimental, and we were in a better place at the end. Within a small community everybody knows each other, which is good and bad. Also, I am direct, and even when I was right, the truth is not always popular. From my perspective, until you can follow, you can't lead because you don't know the value of the gifts of others. I do encourage people to take responsibility and do their piece. And I expect them to. On the plus side, I'm not a micromanager, mostly because I can't deal with explaining a lot of details.

After two and a half years in leadership living in Los Angeles, I found that I was still pining for Oakland and my friends. I made a retreat that year at the Sisters of St. Joseph Spirituality Center in Orange, California. One of the key parts of the retreat was becoming aware of the fact that God was nudging me to give up my pining for Oakland. In fact, what I heard was very direct: "Get over it, Simone." Then I heard that I needed to "get over" not only the loss of all my friends in Oakland, but all the other losses in my life. It was time for change, and it left me breathless. I railed at God: *Give me one good reason! You said losses were the doorways to life! Why should I give up my doorways?* When I finally calmed down enough to listen to an answer, what bubbled up was this: *If you don't have walls, you don't need doorways. The more you hold on to your doorways, the more you hold on to your walls!* That answer caused me to hyperventilate. It left me speechless. It was about a complete change of spiritual life and images. Quite candidly, such a big change made me want to run and hide. I filed it away to nibble on in little pieces when I could. But in the crucible of leadership, I was not prepared for such a big transition.

For me, the takeaway for those five years was the gift of servant leadership. Servant leadership is not about doing things for others necessarily. It's about stripping away the exterior trappings, quite like eating an artichoke. Each leaf removed has a

ing God in the mountains. I said in my mind: *I'll miss you,
God . . . but you are EVERYWHERE*. I was thinking of God as being in all locations. But what came back to me, inside of me like a
thunderclap, was *NO! Simone! I **AM** everywhere*. In that moment I
knew that God is the "hum" that holds all creation together at every moment of existence. God is intimately connected and never
separate. God IS us (but we are not God). It is this insight into
God's living reality that keeps me engaged in this journey. We are
not separate, we are not orphaned. My entire spiritual landscape
was utterly altered and that was gift. All my familiar landmarks
were gone and it was all new.

Initially, as I started doing Zen in the 1980s, I had been inspired by John Henry Newman's famous lines in "Lead, Kindly
Light":

> Lead, Kindly Light, amidst th' encircling gloom,
> Lead Thou me on!
> The night is dark, and I am far from home,
> Lead Thou me on!
> Keep Thou my feet; I do not ask to see
> The distant scene; one step enough for me . . .

But after my walls disappeared, I found that there was no place
to go. It was more a question of being in the midst of the light, in
the midst of the fire—being inspired without being consumed.
So my mantra shifted to Gerard Manley Hopkins, the English
convert (like Newman) and Jesuit priest, and his poem "God's
Grandeur" with its image of shimmering light amid the earthi-
ness and oppression of human existence:

> The world is charged with the grandeur of God.
>> It will flame out, like shining from shook foil;
>> It gathers to a greatness, like the ooze of oil

Crushed. Why do men then now not reck his rod?

Generations have trod, have trod, have trod;

   And all is seared with trade; bleared, smeared with toil;

   And wears man's smudge and shares man's smell: the soil

Is bare now, nor can foot feel, being shod.

And for all this, nature is never spent;

   There lives the dearest freshness deep down things;

And though the last lights off the black West went

   Oh, morning, at the brown brink eastward, springs —

Because the Holy Ghost over the bent

   World broods with warm breast and with ah! bright wings.

Ah! Bright wings! Just as Zen meditation became a path for me to explore spirituality, so too did poetry become a path for higher creativity, as Julia Cameron puts it in *The Artist's Way*. I was reading that book during my sabbatical. I wanted to do photography, but that's an expensive hobby. One day, back while I was general director, I had said to one of my colleagues, in a moment of exasperation, "Oh, how do you work with me?" It was an honest question. I do know myself. She gave a very generous answer: "Oh, it's always interesting working with a poet."

A poet? I'd never thought of myself as a poet. But after Tucson I thought I'd try it as another way to live on the edge of awareness and insight, about myself and about the world. As I wrote in one of my early efforts:

Impetuous me favors the passionate tumult of Spring

River flooding. Sensuous me favors the indolent

Caress of Summer river flowing. Reflective me

Favors the penetrating seep of Autumn river trickling.

Even aloof shy me favors the chilled reserve of Winter

River freezing. But, all of me resists evaporation.

I resist the sucking pulling warn air wresting
me from unknown boundaries. I resist drifting unseen
to unknown parts. I resist the uncertainty of unformed
floating yearning rather to surround rocks, carve
new paths. I resist the ambiguous foggy drift.
But luckily, at times, I am yanked into the air. There

beholding earth's
anguish: Weep!
weeping, raining,
puddling . . . perhaps
the beginning of an
exuberant Spring.

It was the sabbatical that gave me the expansive time to digest the experience of leadership and my life as an attorney. Knowing that God is creating us at every minute allowed me to see the gifts of each moment. Gratitude became the core of my being. So often I saw things that were less than what I would have planned, but they turned into a joyous gift. One example of this was that I took Sister Rochelle (who was like "vice president" when I was the leader of our community) to Europe during the spring of my sabbatical year. The first country we visited was Greece. We went to Delphi (which was a dream of mine), and the museum and upper site were closed because it was a national holiday so we couldn't enter. On the other hand, there were *no* tourists because of that, and we got to wander the temple of Athena with no one else there—an almost unheard-of treat in this tourist destination. Because one part was closed, the other was open and opened up other gifts!

Perceiving these gifts given was the fruit of sabbatical and contemplation. Sometimes I want to give gifts back. But for the most part, on reflection, all these gifts have been surprising, life-giving moments for which I am deeply grateful. Still, in that moment, it took me a while to figure out what the next step was going to be for me. I was listening to the Spirit and trying to discern the path of my ministry. One of our sisters approached me about taking over a program, called Jericho, that we had started in Sacramento to do legislative advocacy for those living at the margins in California. After speaking with the program's board and community leadership, the Jericho job seemed like a good step. It was an extension of the work that I had done previously and the sort of work that actually got me to go to law school in the first place. I had some new experiences and skills to share, and I was willing to give this ministry a try.

As often happens, it was a step that would lead me on to a destination I could never have foreseen.

4

Walking Willing:
Iraq to Washington

A state capitol is really a village, albeit a peculiar village. People seem to think of their legislature as a place set apart in time and space, where the basic laws of economics—such as how much money can go into how many programs based on how much revenue—do not apply. Morality appears to have been suspended as well, kept in some bell jar on a dusty bookcase to show visitors. In reality, however, the dynamics of a legislature wind up being pretty much like those of many villages—or families, or even religious communities. The dysfunction drives you crazy, bad habits die hard, if at all, and trying to get enough people moving in the same direction to accomplish anything seems impossible—until it happens. And all these flaws are distorted by politics, and then magnified by the fun house mirror held up by the media. But at the end of the day we are still talking about people, with all their sins—and occasional virtues—and that's the way I approached my lobbying job in Sacramento.

Jericho was founded in 1987 by Sister Sheila Walsh and Sister Deborah Lorentz, also members of the Sisters of Social Service. The goal of Jericho is to protect and advance the interests of people living in poverty in California by equipping concerned citizens in the interfaith community with tools for advocacy. Jericho's staff also lobbies at the state capitol and in legislative districts for effective structural changes in public policies.[13]

Jericho is the only statewide, interfaith, nonpartisan, grassroots public policy organization in California founded specifically with this mission on behalf of low-income people and families. And of course our organization took its name from the biblical battle that the Israelites won when Joshua led them around the city of Jericho blowing their trumpets until the walls came tumbling down.

That's pretty much what we did, or hoped to do, though usually in more muted tones.

For example, when the news was full of stories about healing through prayer, I thought, *Well, if you can heal illness through prayer, maybe we can heal our government through prayer!* So I recruited retired Catholic sisters to pray for a particular state legislator. First, I gave the sisters who agreed to do this a photo and background information on their assigned legislator. The sister then promised to pray every day for that legislator and his or her staff so that they would be attentive to the needs of all Californians. Each sister sent a picture of herself and her biographical information. Then I took the picture and bio of each sister and went to visit the legislators to let them know that this sister was praying for them, and what they were praying for. These appointments many times became amazing pastoral visits.

Assemblywoman Patty Berg from Eureka was newly elected

when I went to see her. I gave her the picture of the sister who was praying for her and Ms. Berg burst into tears. "This is so hard! This job is so hard!" she cried. It was powerful for me to witness firsthand how difficult it could be to struggle to write bills and turn them into laws—good and just laws. Another legislator, a Catholic, was having such a hard time with his bishop. He was so grateful that I came to visit him and to know that he had "a sister on his side," as he told us. One of our sisters, Rita Meiners, is a wonderful watercolorist. She was praying for Sheila Kuehl, a Democrat who was a senator at the time. Senator Kuehl loved Rita's work so much that she got one of her paintings hung in the state capitol (though it was put in the Republican caucus room, which irritated Sister Rita no end).

One day in early November 2002 I came back to my office after a day of lobbying and there was a voice mail for me from Sister Kathy Thornton, a Sister of Mercy who was then head of NETWORK in Washington: "Hi, Simone, this is Kathy," she started matter-of-factly. "I've got kind of an interesting request, but you need to make a decision in forty-eight hours. Do you want to go to Iraq with me?"

Well . . . Much as I love to jump at a chance for a new experience I paused before answering. It wasn't as though I hadn't traveled before, seen some of the world. After law school, I traveled to Europe for the first time with one of our sisters, and I later visited our founding motherhouse in Eastern Europe where the Sisters of Social Service originated. I had visited our sisters in Taiwan and the Philippines, and I had been to Mexico, representing the Leadership Conference of Women Religious at a meeting in Cuernavaca in 1998. In a more dramatic setting, I represented LCWR as part of a small delegation, just four religious (a priest and a sister from Canada and the United States representing the organizations of leaders of religious communities in both countries), that visited the Mexican state of Chiapas in 1996. We went during the conflict between the Mexican government and the indigenous Zapatista National Liberation Army. We wanted to show our support for the women and men religious—sisters, brothers, and priests—who were deeply involved in helping the indigenous population that had suffered so long and so cruelly at the hands of plantation owners who exploited them and governments who oppressed them.

In San Cristobal, we were also able to visit with Bishop Samuel Ruiz Garcia, who at the time was a crucial figure at the center of the crisis in Chiapas. Don Samuel was a longtime champion of the poor and the indigenous, a saintly and savvy bishop who was first and foremost a pastor. He learned to speak four Mayan languages and would travel by mule around the diocese, which had become a kind of world stage for the fight for social justice in Latin America. Bishop Ruiz Garcia was loved by the people, opposed by the government and business interests, and viewed with suspicion by the Vatican. In an effort to stifle Don Samuel's work, the Vatican named another bishop and conservative theologian, Raul Vera Lopez, to keep an eye on him. Bishop Vera Lopez then confounded Rome by becoming as committed to the cause as Don Samuel was—converted by the people. Of course once converted, the Vatican then decided that Bishop Vera Lopez should not succeed Don Samuel, and Rome instead moved him to the Diocese of Saltillo. Don Raul was so imbued with the Gospel mission that he asked the people not to protest this injustice done to the San Cristobal diocese because he said that in fact the Spirit was using this story to spread the message about the need to care for the poor. To this day, as bishop of Saltillo, Don Raul remains a powerful voice for justice. The Holy Spirit blows where he, or she, will.

When Don Samuel died in 2011, Bishop Vera Lopez compared the man he had been sent to replace to the prophet Jeremiah, "a man who lived and experienced contradiction." What a wonderful epitaph.[14]

Those were all profound experiences for me, but traveling to Iraq was something else altogether. The September 11, 2001, attacks had ratcheted up global tensions to levels that hadn't been seen since the days of the Cold War. After the Bush administration's early reprisals against Afghanistan, all eyes had then turned to Iraq; the White House seemed determined to invade and depose Saddam Hussein, using as its justification the fear of another 9/11 and the argument that Baghdad had weapons of mass destruction. The administration seemed unconcerned that Iraq had nothing to do with the September 11 attacks or that Iraq was in fact not stockpiling nuclear or chemical weapons. The Bush administration had another agenda altogether, and the U.S. Conference of Catholic Bishops, the Leadership Conference of Women Religious, the Conference of Major Superiors of Men (representing priests and brothers in religious orders), and a host of other Catholic organizations and leaders—most notably Pope John Paul II and his representatives—lobbied fiercely against invading Iraq. It would not be a "just war" under Catholic and classic Christian teaching, and we had a duty to do all we could to stop it.

In December 2002, during the planned peace mission, international weapons inspectors were still in Iraq trying to find the "weapons of mass destruction" that in fact did not exist, but it was really a matter of when, not if, the U.S. military would be ordered to attack. Moreover, our small peace delegation of eleven could have been charged by the U.S. government with aiding and abetting the enemy because we were going to spend money in Iraq during our stay. That could have been construed as helping the enemy's economy.

Yes, I was nervous, I admit it. Still, how could I not go? I was doing everything I could to resist the coming war. I had lobbied in DC, demonstrated in San Francisco and Sacramento. How could I not take this next step? In his book *Will and Spirit*, Gerald May says the only thing you bring to the contemplative life is a willing heart. The two things that shut down the contemplative life, as we know from the story of the Transfiguration, are fear and grasping. And so I've come to describe my spirituality as "walking willing." I have to be willing to go where the Spirit leads. Walking the path is the content of the contemplative life. Yet with just forty-eight hours to decide, I had to go through the microwave version of this discernment process. I had to deal with my fear, the concerns of my religious community, the mission of Jericho, and the simple challenge of making a momentous decision quickly. Over the course of a few intense hours I spoke to the president of the board of Jericho and consulted with my community—as well as my conscience—and the answer was quick, and clear: I should go.

We arrived in Amman, the capital of neighboring Jordan, first to be briefed on the situation by Middle East experts. Then, on December 11, 2002, we drove twelve hours across the border to Baghdad; we would visit sites in and around Baghdad and Basra over ten days and leave on December 21. I was not one of the most notable folks on our eleven-member delegation, which included Rick McDowell, a leading opponent of U.S. sanctions against Iraq, as well as Father Roy Bourgeois, a Maryknoll priest and prominent peace activist. Other delegates were David Robinson of Pax Christi, Chuck Quilty of Voices in the Wilderness, Father John Grathwohl of Veterans for Peace, Sister Kathy Thornton and Sister Beth Murphy, a Dominican, and Sister Lil Mattingly, a Maryknoll nun. I wonder if my own relatively low profile may have allowed me to experience the trip so much more powerfully because it was not mediated by organizational concerns. It was just personal.

In Iraq, in that Advent season, on the eve of an invasion by forces from my own country, the human drama was so intense I could not miss a moment of it. I wondered how anyone could, wherever you were. Why we in the United States were so blind to the consequences of our actions baffled me then and pains me deeply to this day.

Perhaps no one wanted to think about it. We were so obsessed with our own anger, our own fear, that we could not see the fear and anguish of others. In Iraq, you couldn't miss it. On our first day there, at an orphanage in Baghdad operated by the Dominican sisters of Iraq, the older orphans were telling the younger ones not to worry because they had lived through the first Gulf War a decade earlier. At a hospital later that day, the mother of a little boy with leukemia pleaded with me to help get him the treatment he needed to survive. The United States had barred the importation of cancer-fighting drugs because they said these drugs could be weaponized by the Iraqi government. At the same time, depleted uranium from U.S. munitions left over from the first Gulf War were linked to a 400 percent increase in the cancer rate in southern Iraq. "You can cure my child, you can get the medicine!" The poor mother was so desperate, and I felt so helpless. Before the war, thanks in part to U.S. sanctions, Iraq had one of the highest rates of infant mortality in the world and one of the lowest rates for overall life expectancy. It was only going to get worse, much worse, in the months—and years—ahead.

We visited hospitals and orphanages and stopped at a sewage treatment plant that, like many water treatment plants that were vital to the daily existence of ordinary Iraqis, was not working properly because the United States had bombed it in the first Gulf War. Then sanctions barred replacement parts from entering the country. Celebrity Sean Penn and peace activist Kathy Kelly were among those at the water plant to highlight the damage that had already been wrought on Iraqis—a small, bitter foretaste of what was to come. We also visited a university where young people were training to be English translators. They were so eager to talk to native English speakers, especially Americans, so they could practice their language skills. And the first question out of one young woman's mouth was: "I hear that Steven Spielberg and Tom Hanks are in favor of invading our country. Is that true? I'll be very disappointed if it is because I admire their work greatly."

At a maternity hospital run by an Iraqi Dominican, Sister Bushra, I stood in the hallway talking with some of the sisters and the mothers. I could not bear to go into the nursery to see the newborns. Only later did I come to see that as my sin of hiding, something I struggled to confess. The tiny infants there couldn't get the medication and nutrition they needed, and pregnant women were coming in to have their babies delivered early, ahead of the bombings that were expected any day. I've always had the responsibility for taking care of little kids, and I could not take care of these children, and I wanted to hide away. To this day I get tears in my eyes when I think of these vulnerable infants, born into a chaotic and violent situation, and that I could not protect any of them from violence perpetrated by my own country.

A couple of days later I wrote a poem about that visit, inspired by what Sister Bushra told us over a tea that the Dominicans organized for our delegation:

> "What will become of them in war?" she cries.
> "My people are my tears."
> O Pilgrims!
> Let Bushra's tears soften your hearts.
> Let Bushra's tears water your relationships.
> Let Bushra's tears melt you into One
> To cry with her, to risk with her the hope:
> Bush would not bomb Iraq
> If he could see our tears.

In one desperate effort to support a family, one mother we met on the streets in Baghdad was taking food storage bags from the

"Oil for Food" program, shredding them, and then crocheting smaller bags that her nephew sold.

As desperate as she was, it was even worse in Basra. I have never seen such destitution as I saw in Basra. Malnutrition and hunger were already commonplace. As we arrived at the house of Basra's archbishop, Gabriel Kassab, a little girl was leaving with a big plate of cooked rice. The archbishop was feeding families out of his home, as many as he could. Here was the Gospel in action. But it seemed to be so little compared to the great need, and the great threat hanging over everyone. In Baghdad we were briefed on the suffering by three aid workers, two women and a man from CARE. One of the women was later abducted and never heard from again and is presumed dead.

While we had to drive overland to get into Iraq, we had to take a plane to get from Baghdad to Basra in the south, though by doing so we would violate the allies' no-fly zone. But provoking hostile fire from an allied fighter jet was the least of my worries. We were flying in an Iraqi Air 727—a Boeing plane, which would have made my dad, a Douglas man, cringe. Worse still was the condition of the jet. My father always said the key to airline safety is maintenance. Iraqi Air hadn't gotten any spare parts in the past twelve years, since the first Gulf War, and it showed. As we took off, the rear end of plane was wagging back and forth like the tail of some great fish. Instead of heading south, though, we kept circling Baghdad as the pilot came out and walked to the rear of the aircraft. A minute later he came back up the aisle shaking his head, and it was back to Baghdad for an emergency landing with fire engines following us down the tarmac.

In due course they got us another plane, but it actually looked to be in worse shape than the first one, with the storage bin doors missing and God knows what else in the guts of the jet. Turns out this was the spare parts plane that they had been cannibalizing to fix the other planes!

With a prayer on my lips, we boarded. I took an aisle seat; next to me was a blank space where the middle seat had been removed. The window seat was occupied by an Iraqi businessman.

As we took off I turned to one of the delegation sitting behind me and said, "I'm nervous."

"Are you nervous about being in my country?" the Iraqi gentleman said to me.

"No, I'm nervous about being in this plane!"

The Iraqi fellow was very kind and reassuring, though, and told me not to worry, that he made the trip every day. Arab hospitality is legendary and we proceeded to have this wonderful conversation during the entire flight—which was a double blessing because it kept me from thinking about the state of the jetliner. It turned out he was an oil geologist, but because of the sanctions that shut down so much of the oil industry he couldn't get a job. Finally he found work carrying government papers daily between Baghdad and Basra. With this one job he was supporting seventeen members of his family. As we talked the shambling jet flew over the ochre-hued country and he pointed out the oil fields below.

His voice grew strangled as he hunched over and turned to me. It was as though he were imparting a terrible secret, or a confession.

"I just want it over, one way or another," he said quietly, painfully. "We are dying slowly. Let it be over soon. Invade us. Get it over with."

Tears pooled in his eyes. "I have a child."

With those words, my mind flashed back to my own father on the day he buried his own daughter, my sister Katy. That very day in Iraq I wrote a poem, "Jesus Wept," about the two of them, my dad and this Iraqi man:

Be assured that fathers weep for children
Lost. Fathers weep for dreams
Destroyed. Fathers weep while the world
Spins on.
O fathers, my fathers stop
This madness, stop this march
To graves and grieving—
Leave the tears unshed.

As our visit progressed it became clear that people who wanted peace were in the ascendancy in the Iraqi government, and people who wanted war were in the ascendancy in the American government. They were going in opposite directions, and the end result was inevitable. I wrote another poem about the "sandstorm of impotence" that we were fighting through in those days. For many in the United States, Saddam Hussein was the only person who lived in Iraq and would be the lone casualty. We knew better; we saw what was going on.

On December 18, 2002, near the end of our trip, we gathered for an interfaith prayer service at St. Joseph's Chaldean Catholic Church in Baghdad. The liturgy included three bishops and representatives from the local mosque; it had been planned by members of the various Christian and Muslim communities in Baghdad. At the service we read a joint letter that called on people of goodwill in the United States to avert the war and spare the innocents who would be sacrificed as "collateral damage."

"Our government suggests that war is the answer to our fears," we said. "But war will never protect us—it will endanger the entire human family. A war against the people of Iraq will slaughter thousands of innocent men, women, and children in a land already devastated by sanctions. A war could also kill and injure countless young Americans. And a war will unleash violent repercussions and terrorist acts that could destroy our world."

Our peace delegation returned home to the United States, to our daily routines. We were far from Iraq, but the Iraqis were never far from my thoughts. Following the trip, I had my first experience of doing a lot of speaking about our experience and the reality that we found in Iraq. Looking back, I realize that was when I started telling stories of what we experienced with the aim of breaking hearts and strengthening our resolve to stop the oncoming catastrophe. I spoke all over California, Oregon, and even up into eastern Washington State. I did my first press interviews and spoke at my first rally. My heart had been broken by the Iraqis and by our U.S. policy as well, and I was passionate about sharing what we had found. My "day job" was still California state policy, but through the crucible of the Iraq conflict, through the experience of having my heart broken, I was finding a new voice to speak for those who could not.

On the day we started bombing, three months after we got back, I was in the middle of giving a talk to a lawyers' group in San Diego, a big navy town. I just burst into tears when I heard the news, standing up there in front of everyone. The faces of the people we had met tormented me. But while tormented, I became more committed than ever to telling our story and touching people's hearts. I found that one of the best vehicles for that was through my poetry.

The war made me publicly poetic. I was still a "puppy poet" and had never written so much poetry as I did during and after that trip, and I had never shared my writing before with more than just a few close friends. On the trip I started sharing my poems in the mornings when our delegation gathered for prayer. The group then usually wanted to e-mail it back to the States as a reflection of what we were seeing and feeling. The e-mails were circulated far and wide, and that made me a public poet without my even realizing it. In fact, my mother and sister Toni who were following the trip on the Internet e-mailed to say that they had cried at the poem of the Iraqi businessman and Dad. It was such a surprise to me because I had never thought about them reading the poems or how they would feel about my perspective. It drew us closer, I realize, as we shared across a vast distance of thousands of miles.

I have often thought back to one of the poems born of Iraq, "Incarnation," that I penned on December 19, 2002, a few days before we welcomed the birth of Christ once more:

> Let us remember on drear distant days
> We are a promised Christmas joy
> We live as one in this fragile gifted life—
> We are the Body of God!

It didn't take long to reach the "drear distant days." The war was indeed all of the anguish that we predicted. If anything, we underestimated the terrible toll that the American invasion would take.

Upwards of 150,000 Iraqis have been killed in the violence since the March 2003 invasion—that we know of—and countless others have suffered from disease and malnutrition and trauma and all the attendant ills wrought by decades of war and international sanctions. The church in Iraq, one of the oldest in Christian history, dating to apostolic times—has been devastated, declining from some 1.5 million Iraqi Christians (many of them Catholics of the Chaldean rite) to fewer than 500,000 today. They continue to flee, as churches are attacked and the economy implodes under the weight of political and societal instability. The United States is not taking in nearly enough of these refugees, nor are we helping to rebuild the country as we should. Instead we are leaving as fast as we can and staying as far away as possible.[15]

Is this how we Americans show we are the Body of God? Do we cut off a limb so blithely?

Also consider what this has done to us here at home: some forty-five hundred American troops were killed and thousands more injured, often grievously so. And those are the visible wounds. So many more veterans are suffering from posttraumatic stress disorder, and suicides among veterans are spiking to record levels, surpassing the number of combat deaths in Afghanistan in 2012.[16]

They fought overseas and they came back to an economy ruined by our own profligacy and skewed priorities. The Bush administration ran our economy into the ground, launching a hugely expensive war without paying for it and passing two tax cuts that primarily benefited the rich. The result: too many of the veterans who went to serve in that war can't find decent jobs for themselves and their families, and the government isn't providing nearly enough support for the men and women who have served so valiantly. And the latest price tag for our military folly? More than $4 trillion, maybe up to $6 trillion, with the largest portion of that bill still coming due, according to one study.

In Washington, meanwhile, conservatives who pushed for this ghastly war and did not pay for it now say we can't afford to take care of our own. I say we can't afford not to.

Iraq changed me, and a little over a year after returning from that country, I had another life-changing opportunity—this time to preach the message I had discovered where it might make an even bigger difference: on Capitol Hill.

I had been a member and supporter of NETWORK almost since its inception, and many people around the country knew me through the national training workshops I would give for priests and brothers and sisters on how to use the law on behalf of people in ministry. The upshot of those workshops: "Mission trumps law." If your lawyer says you can't do something your mission calls you to do, get another lawyer.

Sister Kathy Thornton left NETWORK in 2003 after a very successful tenure as executive director, even though the years after George W. Bush became president in 2000 had not been easy for our agenda. In March 2004, the interim director, Sister Maureen Fenlon, asked me to apply for the job, and I must admit I had mixed feelings. I applied for the post and didn't hear anything until the summer. So for months I didn't know if anything was happening or whether I was even under consideration. Then in early July, I was asked to come to Washington for an interview. I talked with the board's search committee and the staff, but I was still uncertain about whether I wanted to make this move because I was still deeply involved in a range of issues back in California through the work of Jericho.

This was soon after the recall drive that dumped Governor Gray Davis and installed Arnold Schwarzenegger. I organized a "Welcome Wagon" for the new governor in an effort to let him get to know the rest of California, because I thought his experience before politics was way too narrow. He was a movie star and did not know the struggles of people who work hard every day and live in poverty. I had all our social service agency partners around the state write up a one-pager on what they do and who they serve to include in large binder of challenges and state resources. I could never get a meeting with Governor Schwarzenegger, but I developed a good relationship with his Health and Human Services secretary, Kim Belshe. As a result of our first "welcome wagon" meeting, she asked us to make it a quarterly event so that she could get more information about what was happening in the field. I felt that we were making progress on important projects on health care and housing.

After my interview with the NETWORK board in July, there was another few weeks of silence and I figured that door was closed; the decision about whether to stay in California had been made for me. Then in August came the call with the offer. I was still ambivalent. I'm a Californian, after all, and NETWORK was far away from all that I knew. In addition, I had to wonder: In the political climate of 2004, with Republicans in charge of Congress and the White House, could I make a difference? Moreover, was this what I was truly called to do? Then again there were practical considerations. Our religious community, the Sisters of Social Service, is like many religious orders in that we have an aging population and rising costs—like many families. Sister Marti McCarthy and I were both working at Jericho, but money was tight in our organization and we could not afford a good salary for each of us. So we had been thinking about applying for jobs that would pay better—everything we make goes back to the community's common till—in order to help support our sisters and the work the SSS does.

In the end, after consulting with the community, we decided that my taking the NETWORK position was the best thing to do. I negotiated to delay my start date so that I could finish the California legislative session in mid-October, but the decision was made. So it was off to Washington, starting work and this new adventure on November 1, 2004—the day before the November 2 general election, when we elected George W. Bush to a second term—though, as I like to point out, it was the first time we elected him by popular vote.

Everything was new for me.

Capitol Hill is just so much bigger than the statehouse in Sacramento, in every way. In California we had eighty assembly districts and forty senate districts, and the legislature was a village. It was easy to get to know the legislators, and their staff. In Washington, the dynamics are also fundamentally different. Because of the way Republicans have dealt with social issues, trying to downgrade programs by devolving them to the states, all the real policy decisions are made in the states rather than in Washington. Congress is just about funding these days, figuring out how much money is going to go where, so almost all the policy fights turn into money fights.

As always, I saw my job as ministry, and I have continued to view it that way. Sometimes we are successful in what we are trying to do, and sometimes we're not. I tried for four years to get a meeting with President Bush's White House Office of Faith-Based and Community Initiatives, but I could never even get a call returned.

Democrats were understandably more welcoming since we had more in common, policy-wise. That synchronicity has only increased as the Republicans have gone increasingly down the tea party dead end. I wonder when, or whether, the GOP will return to be a party that truly supports business and doesn't simply try to feed off sowing fear. Will they wise up in light of their election setbacks? Or will occasional victories—and inevitable Democratic snafus—continue to blind them to policies that promote the common good and, by the way, would help them politically?

It's not easy being a politician anywhere these days, and especially not in Washington. I can't begin to count up the number of times I have thanked the Lord that I am working for change from the outside of government rather than having to be inside that sausage-making pressure cooker. If you are an elected official, you are always on, and always in demand. And yet so many of them have been sure to make time for me—it helps of course that I'm a Catholic sister, and on their side of an issue. Fairly soon after I arrived at NETWORK, for example, I did a press conference with several Democratic senators—Ted Kennedy, Hillary Clinton, Dick Durbin, Chuck Schumer—about raising the minimum wage. They let me go last—that's known as the "power position" on the Hill! I was amazed. Senator Clinton arrived late, but when she got there, she grabbed my hand and whispered, "I'm going to introduce you!" And afterward people were really touched by what I said. Senator Durbin said, "Sister, you make me so proud to be a Catholic." And then Senator Schumer chimed in and said, "You make me proud to be a Catholic too! Of course I'm not. I'm Jewish."

Are we friends? It is hard to call something friendship in the traditional sense when you are in politics in Washington. For them, they always have to ask, "Who can you trust?" Everyone is angling for something, anything, and all the time. It's isolating. It's so lonely. There are a number of people in Congress who know me well, and who have been wonderfully supportive—for example, Reps. Rosa DeLauro, Marcy Kaptur, and Nancy Pelosi. Before we went out on the bus trip in June 2012, for instance, Leader Pelosi asked to see us, along with Reps. Anna Eshoo and Rosa DeLauro. That was very kind and supportive—solidarity for a shared goal. But it's not exactly friendship. It's still a power relationship, or maybe a nourishing relationship in a limited way at best. After the bus trip, Rep. DeLauro gave a reception for us, and Nancy Pelosi was late. She came in running and said to me, "You haven't spoken yet, have you?" She had to get to the House floor for a vote, but she got the Republican majority leaders to delay it until she could stop by. In October 2013, she even penned a wonderful tribute to me—and above all to the American sisters—in Politico. Her column pegged exactly what we are about, and who we are working for, and what it means for her and for America:

> If there's a single phrase to describe Sister Simone, it is "compassionate conviction." With bravery, with courage, with optimism, she is focused on the common good. She is a champion for the cause of peace and justice. She has the will and the drive to do right.
>
> These are the qualities that define Sister Simone—and

that make her an inspiration to millions of Americans, Catholic and non-Catholic alike. These are the characteristics that remind each of us of our own responsibilities to speak up, to judge others fairly, to defend the rights of the poor and needy.

These are the values that Sister Simone drives home, on a bus and in our communities—and that we should each strive to live by each day, in Congress and in our country.

These were such kind words acknowledging our mission, but often our interactions make me realize that members of Congress don't have many people who nourish them personally beyond being a public figure.

Ted Kennedy was another who welcomed me to NETWORK early on, and he was always supportive of our work. On his seventy-fifth birthday we wanted to return the favor and we invited him over for lunch. He said sure and brought his beloved Portuguese water dog, Splash. It was then I realized that there was a piece of him that was really introverted, and if he had the dog along, then you would go, "Oh, Senator Kennedy, look at the puppy!" And that gave him a buffer space. I said that to him—I am always saying what I think, for better or worse—and he laughed and acknowledged a bit of the truth of it. It was a lovely time, though I must admit that part of the reason we had him over was because we wanted to show him that we weren't just "the nuns' lobby," the way he and many on the Hill thought of NETWORK. We were bigger than the nuns; there were only three of us religious on staff at the time along with about eight lay staff people, some of them non-Catholics.

Anyway, we had lunch with the senator, we had a great time, we took pictures, and then as he was leaving, he said: "I love you all. I love what you do. The nuns' lobby is great."

Okay, we surrendered! If it works as "the nuns' lobby," it works.

As far as our social justice agenda goes, on the one hand, I probably couldn't have picked a tougher time to arrive in Washington. On the other hand, the 2004 election—a dispiriting loss for the Democrats—was also a great opportunity for people of faith to wake up to what we had to offer. In his campaign for president, Sen. John Kerry had not spoken much at all of his faith nor did he encourage others to speak from a faith perspective. This seemed to leave deeply held values out of the campaign conversation. Some Catholic bishops came out strongly against Senator Kerry because of his stance on abortion rights; he was not in favor of the criminalization of abortion and in some dioceses that was taken to mean that voting for Kerry was voting against your faith. This was painful for many, but I know most especially for Senator Kerry.

Still, a central element of the faith community's electoral postmortem was recognizing how much the absence of a progressive faith focus in Democratic politics had hurt the country. Faith had been relegated to a conservative narrative. We needed to get our voice into the media as part of the mainstream message. It was the effort to rectify that situation that helped spawn groups like Faith in Public Life and Catholics in Alliance for the Common Good, and I arrived in time to help create and shape those initiatives. Most of what we had to do was outside the corridors of direct power, and we were committed to being bipartisan. We thought that this was also the best way to get a hearing for our agenda. But it has been difficult when one party is so hard of hearing.

In the summer of 2008, along with Catholics in Alliance for the Common Good, NETWORK organized a first-of-its-kind platform and the Convention for the Common Good in Philadelphia, set for the weekend following the Fourth of July. That was one of our first big successes after I arrived at NETWORK. We gathered together sixteen other national Catholic organizations to work together to recruit "we the people" to speak of the issues of our time and the concerns we had. We then worked together to put on the convention. It came at an auspicious time because the Obama campaign was raising issues about faith in the public square in terms that had not been part of the Democrats' religious conversation in politics for decades.

More than eight hundred delegates from thirty-five states took part in our convention. We had workshops and listening sessions and in the end endorsed a platform that called for action on the economy, health care, immigration, the environment, and building a consistent culture of life. Over two thousand people in forty states contributed to the platform, which we sent to both presidential candidates and national political parties. Folks had put in a lot of work on these statements; it was a dialogue, an organic process. It was great. Sister Helen Prejean, author of *Dead Man Walking* fame, was there, and Bishop Walter Sullivan, retired bishop of Richmond, Virginia, as well as John Sweeney, president of the AFL-CIO. *Washington Post* columnist E. J. Dionne moderated a panel about faith and politics and John Podesta, head of the Center for American Progress, was there as well.

Back then, we didn't want to listen to politicians tell us what they were going to do. We wanted to tell them what they needed to do and then have them respond to "we the people." We wanted to get a Republican and a Democrat to come to Philadelphia. We invited John McCain and Barack Obama, but of course neither came. The Obama campaign did send representatives, and they sent a video of then-Senator Obama. In the video he said that he did not ask for our endorsement, rather he wanted us to know that he endorsed our platform. I was so touched by his generous statement. When Senator Obama had declared his candidacy for president earlier in the year, I immediately supported him. I liked Obama's style—he asked questions and actually listened to the answers. I thought what we needed was a leader who could listen to the people and shape policy based on real responses.

At the convention we also had Democrats like Sen. Bob Casey Jr. of Pennsylvania and Rep. Marcy Kaptur of Ohio, who both addressed the delegates and responded to substantive policy questions. The focus was always on the common good, not just individual agendas.

But even as we tried to be bipartisan, the Republicans didn't make it very easy. We tried and tried to make a contact with the McCain campaign but got nowhere. I had better luck with the Obama campaign because I had come to know some of his staffers years before. I had been on my Zen retreat in December 2006 when it came to me that Senator Obama (Illinois voters had elected him to his first term two years earlier) was lonely and not too connected to a support system in Washington. I thought I should invite him over to dinner, but while trying to set that up some of his aides and my friends came over for dinner at my apartment in January 2007: Joshua DuBois, who would become head of the Faith-Based Office after Obama was elected president; Alexia Kelley, head of Catholics in Alliance for the Common Good; and Mark Linton, who took Joshua's place in Senator Obama's office after Joshua returned to Chicago to work on the presidential campaign. My belief, reinforced by my meditation the previous month, was that we needed to create connections that lead to community and sharing a meal is the best way to do that.

I continued to follow up on those connections after Philadelphia by going to the Democratic Convention in Denver in late August 2008 to be part of a panel about faith and policy that some campaign staff had set up for the delegates. I was a member of a committee on faith that Leah Daughtry, CEO of the 2008 Democratic National Convention Committee and chief of staff to Howard Dean—and a part-time Pentecostal pastor in

Washington—had started as part of the Democrats' new faith outreach effort. But that was me personally, as an individual; I was not there as head of NETWORK.

For me, the focus of our efforts at NETWORK was all about empowering people, getting people to raise their voices. It's about the Constitution, about "We the People." I was trying to get people to engage, to stop being such couch potatoes. Couch potatoes drive me crazy. So does the media coverage that feeds off their viewing habits. I'm convinced that because people spend so much time watching sports, the media uses nothing but sports metaphors (or war metaphors—we spend a lot of time watching war on TV, too) to cover politics. We need new metaphors. We need better media coverage. The problem with the sports metaphor is that it treats politics and democracy like a spectator sport. Political democracy requires engagement, not passivity. "We the people" must be active in the resolution of the problems of our time.

My approach to lobbying is about getting everybody engaged, getting everyone involved. At NETWORK I say that our power is in our people. That is the key ingredient of democracy when you don't have money, and when you are going up against people who do. We aren't a big K Street operation that can wine and dine and donate our way to election victories and political influence. That's not what we're about anyway, as you may have gathered. I have always thought that if we could touch Paul Ryan's heart, then he could change. Conversion is a valid path to change, the best path to change. But fear gets in the way. I think one of the reasons Congressman Ryan reacted so defensively to my stories is that he fears the change.

Conversion? People tell me that's naive. And yet my heart, and the hearts of my sisters, have been profoundly changed by encounters with so many people. How could you not be changed by Margaret Kistler? Or any of the other people from the bus trip? Paul Ryan is not a bad person. It's his policy that is flawed. He doesn't have enough experience. Likewise, the bishops don't set out to be fearful. They just don't have enough experience of real people and their everyday needs. So let's give them some experience! That's why I keep inviting politicians to "come meet my people." The fact is when I come face-to-face with hardworking folks, I am forever changed. I am convinced that we need Medicaid expansion because of Margaret and Catherine's brother, Tom, and Marla's friend Sally. They died because they could not afford insurance. They each left a grieving family behind, and our bishops and politicians need to walk with them and know the anguish of our time.

I am changed by people like Brittany, a student in Philadelphia who is using Pell grants as she becomes the first person in her family to go to college. She was homeless for a few weeks before the dorm opened. Her courage and determination stir my heart and challenge me to a similar commitment.

Bishops and politicians need to know people like Brenda Ann, who has worked as a teacher's assistant for more than fifteen years. But when I met her in the fall of 2012 in Louisiana, she had been homeless since Hurricane Katrina. She was working as hard as she could but could not get a first and last month's rent together to find a place, and even if she could, apartments were scarce and expensive.

I believe that walking with people who are struggling in our country will open our hearts to our better selves. If that's naive, I'm proud of it. Because we have been effective, for the sake of God. Maybe we should all be more naive.

Barack Obama went on to win a historic victory in November of 2008, in large part because he—and his campaign—energized and empowered millions of Americans. If anyone had predicted that he would become president, they probably would have been called naive, at best. Health-care reform, genuine reform, a true overhaul, was one of his top priorities and a key to the long-term economic health of our country, as well as a moral imperative that the Catholic Church and so many others had been pushing for decades. The new president faced so many monumental challenges as he came into office, but broadening access to quality health care while lowering costs was a focus for him—and for NETWORK.

There were so many powerful players involved in this epic battle. But we at NETWORK had no idea how our small organization was going to have the opportunity to help nudge such an important change into becoming a historic reality.

5

Health-Care Reform:
Divided, Not Conquered

In unwinding the ball of yarn that is the past, and in this case the truly tangled past of the fight for health-care reform, we need to recall two foundational realities of the time: a rapidly worsening health-care crisis in the United States and a political environment that was constantly approaching the brink of a complete meltdown. Remember the atmosphere at the time, when President Bush was in the third year of his second term. I had worked against many of his policies on the domestic front—dismantling the safety net, tax policy that favored the extremely wealthy, and the like—and internationally, on Iraq and Afghanistan. We had tried to collaborate on immigration reform, but the Bush administration did not know how to do that effectively. I never got any call back from the White House's faith-based office, and the stonewalling led to a great deal of pent-up frustration.

Barack Obama's election in November 2008 represented a great new opportunity for NETWORK and the agenda of Catholics and other religious progressives who had been working for years to limit the damage caused by the Bush administration—and now could work to promote constructive changes. Chief among those was health-care reform.

Our Convention for the Common Good in Philadelphia in July 2008 had asked all the participating groups to submit their top three concerns for enhancing the common good, and we pulled them together and set them out in the context of the preamble to the Constitution—trying to form a more perfect union. The top five platform issues were: health-care reform, the economy, immigration reform, peace building in Iraq and Afghanistan, and the environment.

This platform was used across the country by hundreds of groups. We did a panel presentation at the Democratic Convention, and while we were unsuccessful in our attempt to present it at the Republican Convention, the platform became for many a touchstone for a faithful way forward. Once the election was over, the top five issues became the focus of our work at NETWORK for the next four years. Health care was the first big issue to be engaged by Congress, so we were well positioned to advocate on this issue, knowing that it was of critical importance to our members.

It was also vital to the health of the nation. Consider some of the key problems fueling the urgent need for reform:

- Almost fifty million people lacked any form of health-care insurance, and the number was rising. As the recession was deepening and people were losing their employment, they were also losing their health-care coverage. Margaret Kistler, Sally, Tom, and millions of others could not afford coverage in the private market and had nowhere to turn. All three died prematurely without care. This is wrong in the richest nation on earth.

- Employer costs for health-care premiums were rising rapidly, with no end in sight. This rapid rise resulted in many employers either dropping health-care coverage as a benefit or requiring employees to pay some of the insurance premium out of their salaries. Additionally, employers were opting for insurance coverage that had higher co-pays and deductibles in order to bring premium costs down. We at NETWORK knew this problem all too well! Over the five years I had been at NETWORK, our premiums had gone up a total of 75 percent. This was much more than inflation, and we as a small organization dependent on donations were having a hard time keeping up with these costs. We were reluctant to pass additional costs on to our staff because we also were not getting any raises (even cost of living) in the recession.

- This impact on employers was limiting U.S. companies' global competitiveness because they had to charge higher prices in order to cover these escalating costs. It should be noted that the United States is the only developed nation in the world that has an employer-based health-care insurance system that is completely private pay. All other developed nations have some form of national health insurance where at least a significant portion of the cost is covered by the state. I was told by a staff member with the Ford Motor Company that he thought the American automobile industry could be much more competitive if companies did not have to solely bear the cost of health insurance. Many employees were actually for more of a "Medicare for all" model of coverage as being the most cost-effective.

- People with insurance and significant illnesses (e.g., cancer) were losing their insurance coverage because they had reached their "lifetime cap" on benefits. When they tried to get other coverage, the disease for which they needed coverage was excluded as a "preexisting condition." Additionally, insurance companies were "cherry-picking" young healthy individuals for insurance coverage and then denying them payment of claims when they submitted medical bills for any illness. The basis for the denials was usually claiming that there was a preexisting condition that the person had not disclosed—whether the individual knew about it or not. A family I met in late 2010 told me that their disabled son had used all of his lifetime coverage by the time he was three years old. What were they going to do? They did not have enough resources to pay for his needs out of pocket, and they did not qualify for other programs for him. They were frantic.

- Medical bills became a leading reason for personal bankruptcy, as more people without insurance were being charged high nonnegotiated fees that they had no hope of paying. In St. Louis I met a family who had lost everything, including the home they owned, in trying to pay the medical bills from cancer treatment for Cynthia, the mother/wife. Their insurance was insufficient to cover treatment, and the bills were astronomical. They did their best, but bankruptcy was their only way for a fresh start.

- Insurance companies were using fewer premium dollars to pay for their policyholders' health-care bills. Rather, they were using more money for salaries and bonuses to top executives, dividends to shareholders, advertising costs, and other administrative costs. In fact, testimony at Capitol Hill hearings indicated that some insurance companies were using 40 to 45 cents of every premium dollar for administrative costs. This is compared to Medicare's administrative cost of 4 to 5 cents of every health-care dollar.

This comparison of administrative cost to health-care dollar is called the "medical loss ratio." That more and more health-care premium money was going to pay high CEO salaries and to Madison Avenue ad agencies to advertise for more business was shocking to me. The pressure on claims representatives to deny claims was extremely high. In fact, when I had injured my wrist before coming to Washington, I had to appeal a denial of my claim for services I very much needed. I even ended up in a telephone hearing to insist on getting the therapy to restore any mobility to my right wrist. Since I was right-handed, I found this need to be pretty basic to my everyday life.

· More uninsured people were going to hospital emergency rooms for treatment because the hospital emergency rooms have a statutory mandate to never turn away anyone as long as the facility has physical space. Thus ERs had to treat more and more sick people who had no coverage and no doctor of their own. Hospitals then apportioned this cost across the rest of their billings. In congressional hearings some estimated that up to 25 cents of every premium dollar was going to cover the cost of the uninsured. The costs were so high because emergency rooms are the most expensive way to get care, *and* people delayed coming and were therefore sicker than if they had gone to their own doctor earlier. In Texas in the summer of 2013, we heard the story of a construction worker who put off going to the ER because of a "pain in his side." He thought that he had just pulled a muscle on the job, but he didn't go to the doctor since he did not have health-care coverage as a day laborer. By the time he got to the ER by ambulance, he had a ruptured appendix and peritonitis had set in. He was in ICU for days and off work for months while he recovered.

Under the principles of Catholic social teaching, this national, systemic failure to meet the rights of citizens to health care demanded a national, systemic response. It was not possible to fix the problems at the individual, local, or even the individual state level.

NETWORK had the expertise and experience to be an important voice in this struggle. We had worked on health-care reform since NETWORK's inception, a four-decade period that also tracked the national debate over health-care reform. Our first newsletter in September 1972 included a lengthy article about the issues then being discussed in Congress about expanding health-care coverage, and we pushed the issue every year after that. In the 1990s, our lobbyists worked with then First Lady Hillary Clinton in President Clinton's effort to address the broken health-care system in our nation.

Health-care reform was also consistent with our constant reference to the social teaching of the Catholic Church to guide our mission. This body of work stresses the dignity of each individual and the view that human beings are social creatures. Because of that, we are bound to one another and cannot live solitary lives in isolation. Rather, we live in solidarity with each other. Repeatedly, popes have stressed the shared responsibility of all to create the common good with a special concern for those people who live in poverty. They point out that all have both an obligation and a right to participate in creating this common good in a just society. In this participation, everyone's work has equal dignity whether they are a day laborer or a CEO of a Fortune 500 company.

The justice component of health care has been a core element of Catholic social teaching—and the work of the Catholic Church in the United States—for decades. In spring 1974, for example, Sister Carol Coston, OP, then executive director of NETWORK, testified on Capitol Hill about the need for comprehensive health-care reform. She cited Pope John XXIII, who in his 1963 encyclical, *Pacem in Terris*, stated clearly that health care is a fundamental right.

More recently, on November 18, 2010, Pope Benedict (who retired in February 2013) issued a statement that reiterated that health care was a right of every person and that "justice in healthcare should be a priority of governments and international institutions." This statement builds on the points in the encyclical where he stresses that the Gospels and Catholic tradition demand that Christ's followers live out both the commutative (personal) justice and the distributive (societal) justice in this challenging call to love. He notes that there is no dichotomy—it is all about love.

In my experience in the Catholic Church in the United States, it seems that we usually split these two aspects of the one command to love. Often, some people tout the antiabortion message as the litmus test of being Catholic, while others use the social gospel and care for the poor as the test. In the encyclical *Charity in Truth*, Pope Benedict says that they are integrally connected and cannot be separated. I personally find this challenging. When faced with someone who is adamant on one side, I have a compulsion to balance things out and take an adamant position on the other. It is my spiritual practice to try to remember, as the encyclical notes, that all of this Gospel life is based in love. I try to open my heart to all people and not get caught in the quagmire of thinking that my insights are better, more right. It is in this context of religious principles and spiritual practice that I experienced the process of health-care reform.

But many Catholic politicians disagree about how all of this gets interpreted. Congressman Ryan, for example, highlights the aspect of individual responsibility in Catholic social teaching. What he misses, however, is that this is only one element of our tradition. The other key part is that this responsibility can only be exercised in the context of community. Many respond that a communal orientation is "socialism." Well, they are wrong. I learned from our sisters in Central Europe who grew up under socialism that centralized planning is very different from shared responsibility. From them I learned that the role of Catholic social teaching is to offset the excesses of any society. For us in the United States, the excess is individualism, so the antidote is communal solidarity. In Central Europe, the excess has been the role of the community in the guise of the state. In that context, Catholic social teaching lifts up the importance of individual responsibility. Each society has something to learn from our tradition—but it might not be the aspect that politicians want to highlight.

Health-care policymaking was a process that, as most will remember, was terribly fraught and politically perilous and had the potential to divide my Church as much as my country. And for many, health-care reform remains a wedge issue. From the start I had to approach the battle from my contemplative stance of "walking willing." This means that I am willing to walk in the dark and respond to needs as they arise. I trust that I will be led and will not be left an orphan. This life of living "yes" grows out of the awareness as St. Paul says that we are one body. If I as one cell of that body am called upon to do something for the body and I can do it, how can I say no? So my contemplative practice of walking willing leads to the asceticism of living yes. What I have discovered is that as long as I focus on the response to need, I have plenty of energy for this life of yes. When I get preoccupied with myself, then my energy wanes, as do my insights and spiritual practice. The challenge is to look outside myself and connect again with the deeper truth of the Holy Mystery in my life.

This spiritual practice has greatly enriched my life and at times has made me nervous. My experience of the health-care debate was a gift of this spiritual practice and a call to which I tried to be faithful.

From the start, our focus was on affordability and access. Affordability was essential for the Margarets, Sallys, and Toms of our nation who have nothing left for health-care costs from their minimum wage paycheck or unemployment check. Low-wage workers are the most likely to not have health care offered as a benefit of employment. So we lobbied in the House and Senate to make sure that working poor and unemployed people in our nation would finally have access to health care.

Throughout the spring and summer of 2009, we spent countless hours on the Hill, lobbying House and Senate members and staffers, monitoring congressional hearings on the bills that were being held in both houses, and praying that Republican opposition—which was strong from the outset and grew implacable as the process progressed—could be overcome. Whatever emerged deserved a vote, an open debate, not death by filibuster.

The element that began to unite Republicans in their opposition was the individual mandate to ensure that everyone had health insurance and no one who could pay would skip out on insurance and leave it to the rest of us to bail them out when they got sick. Even though this individual mandate started as a GOP proposal, in the congressional debate for the GOP, this became an unconscionable, and unconstitutional, infringement on personal liberty. To most of us, it was simply the way insurance worked—if everyone is insured, insurance is cheaper and everyone receives better health care, and greater peace of mind. The mandate—which the Supreme Court would later deem constitutional—was a tax to be shared according to one's ability to pay, just like so many other things we do as individuals in a society. What the opposition missed was the testimony that at least 17 or 18 cents of every health-care dollar was going to cover the uninsured. This meant that the cost of the ICU treatment for the man in Texas with a ruptured appendix and peritonitis was being passed on to those with insurance. It would be much better for all of us if we could each pay a smaller amount and make sure that everyone had coverage.

The opposition did not see it this way, naturally. The high-powered Capitol Hill lobbyists for the health-care industry were aided by the emergence of grassroots, tea party–led opponents who made their case in angry, high-decibel "town hall" meetings with congressional representatives. The exchanges in those meetings, the outrage voiced by citizens who were usually misinformed about the realities of health care and the proposals before Congress, went viral every day and made our job that much harder.

Those of us on the progressive side of the debate were already hampered by the early abandonment by Democrats and the White House of a "single-payer" approach to health care, like the popular and successful Medicare system. We knew that a Medicare-for-all system was the most cost-effective model for providing service. It eliminated much of the administrative cost and historically demonstrated high-quality care. However, when negotiations started in Congress, the Medicare-for-all advocates were not included, in an apparent effort to signal that this process was about a centrist solution and a new sort of politics. Thus the progressive edge and energy was excluded from the debate. This moved the starting point to the right and alienated many activists. The Republicans, who had suffered significant defeats in the 2008 election, were not in a mood for a new politics and were focused on doing everything in their power to regain control. This meant that they were not interested in coming together to solve the nation's problems. Their priority was high-conflict politics as usual.

In hindsight, I believe that it was a mistake to not have the Medicare-for-all position at the table because it gave away a valid point of view without getting something from Republicans in return. Rather than acknowledge that an important point had already been compromised, Republicans took the new starting point as the extreme and bargained from there. As a result, because the middle was taken by the Republicans as the new left, the final bill was much more free market oriented than I believe it would have been otherwise.

But we at NETWORK of course still pressed on. Our goal was to pass a health-care reform bill of significant scope that would begin to reform the ramshackle, unjust system that had existed for decades and that was growing more untenable and unaffordable every year. But as the debate lurched forward through the fall of 2009 and into the winter, the drama focused on whether any bill would ever come up for a vote.

Moreover, as the final act approached its conclusion, abortion became the unlikely issue on which the fate of health-care reform would hinge, and the pivotal players in this drama were all Catholics—the bishops, we sisters, and the Catholic politicians on both sides of the aisle in the House and Senate. The moment proved to be an x-ray that exposed the fissures in American Catholicism.[17]

The crux of the issue was whether the final bill would allow for taxpayer funding of abortions through the proposed health-care reform bills.

In early November 2009, the House passed its version of health-care reform, which included an amendment crafted by Rep. Bart Stupak, a Michigan Democrat, and Rep. Joe Pitts, a Pennsylvania Republican, both of whom were identified as pro-life Catholics. The amendment essentially reproduced the generic ban on federal funding of abortion, called the Hyde Amendment, which has controlled federal spending provisions since the late GOP representative Henry Hyde first introduced this annual practice in 1974. It prohibited the use of federal funds "to pay for any abortion or to cover any part of the costs of any health plan that includes coverage of abortion" except in cases of rape, incest, or danger to the life of the mother.

The health-care reform version of Hyde's language came to be known as the Stupak Amendment because Stupak was the leader of some fifteen to twenty pro-life Democrats whose votes would determine the success—or failure—of the health-care reform bill. The large and powerful contingent of pro-choice Democrats in the House (and Senate) were not at all happy about this blanket ban being applied to the sweeping overhaul of the nation's health-care system, because they believed it could have many unintended consequences. But they figured the language would be modified when the bill was reconciled with the Senate version, and they ultimately decided that the greater good by far was passing a reform bill.

Stupak worked closely throughout the process with staffers from the Catholic bishops conference, the USCCB, which gave their tacit approval to the House version. Despite strong pro-life language in the bill, not a single Catholic Republican backed the House version of health-care reform, which was hailed as one of the most pro-life pieces of legislation in our nation's history.[18]

In December 2009, on Christmas Eve, the Senate passed its version of health-care reform, though barely, and only after strong language against abortion funding drafted by Sens. Bob Casey and Ben Nelson was accepted by a filibuster-proof majority.

For many abortion opponents, the Senate version of the bill was not as clear-cut on the funding ban as the House version, but most of us were confident that both House and Senate versions were plainly consistent with past practices in federal legislation that barred taxpayer funding for abortions. The language in both bills was quite similar to that used for decades to address pro-life concerns, and we advocates figured anything that needed to be added or clarified could be done so when the House and Senate versions were reconciled in committee.

Fate had other ideas. The preceding August, Sen. Ted Kennedy, our friend and a great champion of health-care reform, had died after a long and poignant struggle with brain cancer. His passing deprived the Democrats of a 60-vote majority in the Senate—a key threshold because Democrats needed 60 votes out of 100 to be able to stop a filibuster that would put a halt to any legislative action. Republicans had vowed to use the filibuster to kill health-care reform, much as they have used it to halt a variety of actions and appointments during President Obama's term in office.

The implacable obstructionism of the GOP meant that the special election to fill Kennedy's seat would be critical to keeping the legislative momentum for health-care reform. Yet on January 19, 2010, Massachusetts voters went to the polls in a special election to replace Senator Kennedy and they elected Scott Brown, a Republican, to fill Kennedy's seat. Although Brown was pro-choice, pro-lifers backed him to the hilt because he campaigned on a vow to block health-care reform—a reform that would not affect Massachusetts and was in many ways modeled on the successful Massachusetts version that had been promoted by Republican Mitt Romney when he was governor of the Bay State. Romney would later try to distance himself from that law, however awkwardly, and would go on to lose to Obama in the 2012 presidential campaign. Scott Brown lost his seat in 2012 to Elizabeth Warren, who is much more in the mold of Ted Kennedy.

But all that mattered in January 2010 was that Brown had won and deprived Senate Democrats of a filibuster-proof majority. With that one change, the entire health-care landscape changed.

Very quickly it became clear that the only way forward was to have the House pass the Senate bill. There could be no more tweaking of the bill to reconcile the differences between the House and Senate versions because any new version would have to return to the Senate for a vote, and Republicans there had vowed to vote down anything, even if it contained the stronger abortion funding ban that they wanted.

As a sign of their priorities in the health-care fight, the U.S. Conference of Catholic Bishops (USCCB) had assigned all final policymaking on the legislation to the conference's office on "Pro-Life Activities." That office was not only focused on the single issue of abortion, but it was largely staffed with political conservatives who had long expressed opposition to Obama's policies on a range of issues.

The Catholic Health Association, which was led by Sister Carol Keehan and represents the hundreds of Catholic health-care facilities across the nation—caring for 15 percent of all patients seen in hospitals each year—was also a major player. Sister Carol also worked on the issue of abortion as well as the questions of practical functionality for hospitals and other care providers. This created a complementarity among advocates from a Catholic perspective. Historically, NETWORK has never worked on the abortion issue. We have always been focused on the economic issues and that remained our priority in our work on health care.

Finally, in the beginning of March 2010, House Speaker Nancy Pelosi's office indicated that the Democratic majority was ready to bring the Senate health-care bill to the floor for a vote the week of March 15, 2010.

On Saturday evening, March 13, 2010, the Catholic Health Association issued Sister Carol Keehan's statement endorsing House passage of the Senate health-care bill. I was in Los Angeles for meetings with my religious community and I read the statement the next morning. I immediately e-mailed Sister Carol to let her know that we at NETWORK were standing with her and we put a statement to that effect on our website a few hours later.

I was then pondering and praying about what else we could do to support Sister Carol's position. We often do what we call "sign-on letters," where we get various organizations to sign on to letters that we write in order to demonstrate a broad level of support. It came to me that a sign-on letter by leaders of Catholic women religious congregations could be beneficial because so many congregations have experience in providing health care in our nation. I then drafted a letter and on Sunday evening in Los Angeles, I sent it to the Leadership Conference of Women Religious (LCWR) and all the leaders of women religious congregations that I had in my personal contacts list. I invited their participation and asked these women to share the letter with other leaders. I acknowledged that there was a short time frame because we would have to have their signatures back by the close of business on Tuesday, March 16. That left them a mere forty-eight hours to process it through what is sometimes extensive communal processes. I thought that if we could get twenty signatures in this short time frame, we could "go public" with our letter.

On Monday I was still in California at my community meetings, and in the midafternoon I got a call from a White House contact who told me that the president of the USCCB, Cardinal Francis George of Chicago, had come out in opposition to the Senate bill. Cardinal George's statement said that he took this position principally because he did not think that there were adequate safeguards for the unborn in the bill. Additionally, USCCB staff told Congressman Bart Stupak that they did not trust President Obama to follow the requirements for segregated funding.

Ordinarily, I get disturbing information affecting my work when I am in the office. Then I take a deep breath, stay in a problem-solving mode and try to figure a way forward. However, this news came to me while I was with my sisters. I was home and did not have the armor of the office and my workaday routine to protect me. I came back to the meeting with the other sisters and burst into tears. The only thing going through my mind was that health-care reform was once again dead. I thought of the millions of people who would go without access to medical care and the tens of thousands who would die unnecessarily each year. My sisters responded as family does: with support and concern. They joined me in worry and prayer and gave me hugs and offers of consolation.

Our meditation in those hours became even more intense than usual and filled with cries of "help," "Come, Holy Spirit," and offers to walk willing—but without much of an idea of just what to do. I promised the Spirit that I would do my best to stay open to nudges and to listen deeply to how to move, but we clearly needed help. I did not know how it would end, but I was willing to do my part, in the dark. I was following the path of our "normal" activity and was asking that it be used for the greater good. I do not think that God has favorites, but I do believe that "all things work toward the good." What I am called to do is to walk willing and to live yes.

On Tuesday night, March 16, I took a red-eye flight from Los Angeles back to Washington. I got into the office around 7:00 A.M. Wednesday morning and had the dreamy thought that maybe I would go home early that day because I had not had much sleep on the plane. The first thing I did was to check and see who had signed our "sign-on" letter and discovered that fifty-nine leaders had signed on. That in and of itself was a miracle! It was a ray of hope, and something concrete to work on rather than focusing on how dire the cause looked. By noon, the letter was ready to release to the media. I did many media interviews and within twenty-four hours the story of the sisters' support for the health-care reform bill—in contrast with the bishops' opposition—began to explode.

NETWORK staff e-mailed the sisters' letter to all House offices and then hand-delivered hard copies to the offices of Democrats who are Catholic. We thought that they would be most interested in the position of Catholic sisters, and they would best understand the role that we have played in health care in the United States. In some offices, staffers only coolly accepted our letter. However, in the majority of the offices we went to, we were welcomed enthusiastically; in several cases we were ushered into the congressperson's office. Ohio Rep. Tim Ryan came out to meet us and gave me a big hug. He and his staff were so grateful. They told me that they did not think the Senate bill allowed for federal funding for abortion, but they acknowledged that it would have been difficult to vote for the bill in the face of the USCCB's opposition. The letter of support from the Catholic sisters gave legislators like Congressman Ryan another perspective—and political cover—that allowed them to vote for a bill that would provide care for an estimated thirty-two million people who did not have access to health care, and at the same time maintain the ban on federal funding of abortion.

In addition to speaking with members and staff in congressional offices, I was doing a lot of press interviews. I remember sitting out in the plaza of the Rayburn House Office Building talking on my cell phone with a reporter from the *Los Angeles Times*. He asked me if we were having a fight with the bishops. I said that this was not about a difference within our faith, this was about the application of our faith to politics. I had read the bill as a lawyer, and I believed the plain reading of the bill showed that there was no federal funding for abortion. I told him that I did not think we were having a fight. After a pause I added, "I hope."

This is where my spiritual journey takes center stage. As always when I am in the media spotlight, I face my anxiety by taking a deep breath and praying, "Come, Holy Spirit." I trust as always that I will not be left an orphan. Print journalism is easier for me because I feel like I can explain myself better and do not have to get my message into twenty-second sound bites. Luckily, in February 2010 I had been to a two-day media training that included video interviews with critique and suggestions. While the content had been on immigration, I applied the learning to this explosion of media interest in health care.

Still, the media blitz wasn't easy. I did thirty-three interviews in five days, and easily the most challenging media appearance was going on the Neil Cavuto show on Fox News. Fox is of course noted for its alignment with conservative and Republican causes and is notably not a fan of President Obama or major Democratic proposals—to put it charitably. Fox interviewers can at times be very tough on, even dismissive of, their guests. But for me, because I try to embody the discipline of "walking willing" and living the "asceticism of yes," I had to respond and go on the program when invited. Although I was nervous, my "Come, Holy Spirit" mantra got me through—I was able to make my points and to engage Neil Cavuto while remaining respectful. I thought of this as important "missionary work" so that others who did not hold my same political viewpoint could hear how we approached the legislation and why we thought it was an important step forward for our country.

One question I remember Mr. Cavuto asking was if the sisters, in signing the letter in support of the health-care reform bill, were weighing the needs of those without health care against the needs of the unborn. I immediately said "Oh NO!" I went on to explain that we did not have to choose because we had both. The unborn were protected *and* those without care would get it. This wound up as a profound experience of faith for me—I felt I did not have to be afraid, and the Spirit gave me words that expressed just what we wanted to say. Otherwise I might have fallen into the temptation of either/or thinking that makes for more conflict and misunderstanding.

The bishops were in serious either/or mode, as it happened, and were issuing some of the most forceful denunciations of the health-care bill that we had ever heard. At the very least, the tone and content of their absolute language did not reflect any of the nuance that any piece of legislation as large and complex as this one will have. Making a prudential judgment on a bill, in humility and based on the various legal and political interpretations available, was one thing. Declaring, as the bishops seemed to be doing, that one must oppose a bill like this to in effect be a good Catholic, and in the face of so much expert legal and ethical reasoning to the contrary, was confounding.

Many international media outlets were interested in this story because they said it was the first time that they knew of in which contrasting positions, on such a prominent issue, were taken by two respected sectors of Church leadership—the sisters and the bishops. I said in response that we were each about our mission. The mission of the bishops, as I see it, is to protect the institution of the Church from prospective dangers and feared possibilities. The mission of Catholic sisters is to respond to the present needs of people around us. In this instance that meant getting health care for more than thirty million people and protecting the unborn.

The final hours before the bill was brought to a decisive vote were as tense as anything I have ever experienced in political life. Bart Stupak said he would not bring his cohort on board unless the Catholic bishops were satisfied that the bill would bar abortion funding. All sorts of guarantees were made, but nothing was sufficient for the bishops' staff.

Finally, President Obama personally issued an executive order declaring that no federal funds would be used for abortions under the law. It was the same kind of language that President Bush had used to bar federal funding for embryonic stem cell research, for example, and it represented a great moment of triumph. Stupak was satisfied and called the USCCB staffers to give them the news. But suddenly they wouldn't even take his calls. The bishops' staff, it seems, wouldn't take yes for an answer.

Stupak and the pro-life Democrats were on their own. They decided to vote for the bill anyway, believing—correctly—that it barred funding for abortion. Their votes put the Affordable Care Act over the top.

Finally, on Sunday evening March 21, 2010, the bills were coming to the House floor. Congressman Tim Ryan and his fellow Ohioan and pro-life Democrat, Rep. John Boccieri, escorted three of us from NETWORK to the gallery so that we could watch the historic vote. On the way, they introduced us to several of their colleagues as "the ones who wrote the nuns' letter." I was embraced, thanked, and welcomed by many. It was such a profound honor to be in the gallery when the House voted to adopt Senate bill H.R. 3590—technically known as the Patient Protection and Affordable Care Act, or PPACA (also ACA), and colloquially called "Obamacare." That last one is a label I think the president will wear proudly, though his opponents used it as an epithet.

Increasingly it became clear that our sign-on letter had been one of the critical factors in tipping the balance for a yes vote for this groundbreaking reform. Some said it helped solidify or bring in as many as two dozen votes. Later I was asked how I had so effectively timed the sisters' letter. I had to say that as a person of faith, while I would like to claim credit for being so politically astute, it really was the Spirit's work and not mine.

Two days later, on Tuesday, March 23, President Obama signed the bill into law at a White House ceremony and celebrated at the Department of the Interior auditorium. I was honored to be in the audience at the Department of the Interior, and as I introduced myself to the president, he hugged me and said that our letter was the tipping point in the struggle. Vice President Biden also gave me a big hug and, in his typically exuberant way, called me "his nun" and said that the sisters were part of the reason he was still Catholic. It moved me deeply to have this affirmation of NETWORK's efforts over nearly four laborious decades. It was all worth it, every bit. I felt that I was standing on the shoulders of all of our "foremothers" in celebrating this extension of the right to decent and affordable health care. In being faithful to the Gospel and our mission, we had helped accomplish something critically important for our nation and especially for those who do not have access to care. For me this was a vibrant expression of Pope Benedict's idea of "distributive justice." No more Margarets, Sallys, or Toms should die in our nation unnecessarily. We had made change for them. That made my heart happy.

Not every reaction was so positive. We and the other signers of the letter received hundreds of calls calling us "baby killers" and telling us that we were not really Catholic. We received hate mail and threats. One bishop told a signer that her congregation could not use diocesan property for their annual social justice meeting. Another bishop told a congregation that supported the ACA that they could not advertise their vocation day in their diocesan paper. Our relationship with the USCCB was seriously strained but so far not permanently ruptured, which is vitally important since we collaborate on other important issues.

Many people have told me that our work on health-care reform was a very prophetic stance. I am deeply honored by that view, but surprised that being prophetic could be so messy. It is still a matter of walking in the dark, it seems, making mistakes and trying to do the best that we can. For me this is the essence of the spiritual journey—taking our Gospel faith and Church's teaching into the marrow of our being and trusting that in our willingness we will be used so that all things work to the good.

As Thomas Merton said:[19]

We must never forget that Christianity is much more than the intellectual acceptance of a religious message by a blind and submissive faith which never understands what the

message means except in terms of authoritative interpretations handed down externally by experts in the name of
the church. On the contrary, faith is the door to the full inner life of the Church, a life that includes not only access to
an authoritative teaching but above all to a deep personal
experience which is at once unique and yet shared by the
whole Body of Christ, in the Spirit of Christ.

That was the Spirit. But politics, especially in our polarized
nation at this point in our history, is another thing altogether.

In some respects, we at NETWORK were rather naive about
the reality of the midterm elections in the spring and fall of 2010.
We were exhausted after the grueling health-care fight. I think
we thought that because we had won the '08 election, and the
health-care battle, we could rest. It was a bad time to let our fa-
tigue take over and to fail to rally for the 2010 campaign, but that
is exactly what happened. While we celebrated the law's passage,
the frightened right-wing fringe organized and mobilized for the
2010 midterm elections.

The results were disastrous. The House of Representatives
went to the Republicans, and even more important was that state
houses and governors' mansions across the country went to the
GOP, and the right wing of the party at that. Just as bad, pro-life
Democrats were decimated, pilloried by Republican candidates
who said the Democrat candidates had supported abortion in the
ACA. Subsequent events and court rulings have shown that our
position on the health-care law's safeguards against abortion
funding were correct, but it was too late. Stupak retired, and ap-
proximately half of the members of the Democrats for Life Caucus lost in the polls.[20] Our friend Congressman Tim Ryan from
Youngstown, Ohio won, but other friends, like Tom Perriello and
John Boccieri, lost.

Moreover, 2010 was a census year when congressional and

state legislative districts were redrawn to reflect the current de-
mographic reality. Over the years this has become an exercise in
creating "safe" seats for each party. Since the governor and legislature of each state sets the voting district boundaries, when
many state legislatures and governorships went Republican in
2010, the GOP was able to run the redistricting process. This resulted in entrenching a Republican majority in the House of Representatives, perhaps until the next census and the 2022 election.
It is worth noting that Democratic candidates actually got a million more votes in 2012 than the combined total of the Republican
candidates. But the Republicans rule the House because of how
those district lines were drawn.

In the 112th Congress that began in January 2011, the House of
Representatives spent its time in vain efforts to repeal the Affordable Care Act or to defund it. It was horrifying for the NET-
WORK staff that legislators should be so ignorant of the basics
of civics. Every time the Republican leadership wanted to stir
up their members in the House, they again proposed the repeal
of the ACA. They did it over forty times, even though they knew
that it was not going anywhere as long as there was a Democratic-
led Senate and a Democrat in the White House. Their action was
about politics, not policy.

It is this division that is more interested in the political game
and less interested in actual governance that is contributing to
gridlock in Congress. Evidenced in the struggle over the economy,
the Ryan budget, the debt standoffs and fiscal cliffs, and myriad
other issues, this perverse dynamic has made it immensely more
challenging for us as we try to actually accomplish anything.

As one of our first actions in early 2011, we at NETWORK
began to prepare a campaign about income and wealth disparity in our nation that we called "Mind the Gap." Over Christmas
break many of us read the book *Spirit Level*[21] and found it disturb-

ing that the 100 percent were suffering in our nation because of the widening gap. This brought the growing disparity front and center for us six months before the "occupy" movement took off. In fact, we delivered a petition to Jon Carson in the West Wing of the White House calling on the administration to hold a summit on this growing income divide. Our petition was signed by over 7,000 of our members and was a portent of things to come. I realize now that this work helped to lift up the issue and move it into the public consciousness. It took longer than we thought, but now that the issue is front and center, I am proud to point to the groundwork that we did three years ago to make it happen.

A second action occurred when Congressman Paul Ryan first proposed his budget. We at NETWORK came together and established a concerted lobbying strategy to push back against it as a framework for our nation. We were instrumental in getting the interfaith community organized and together we prayed daily out in front of the Methodist building across the street from the Capitol and the Supreme Court. We did "grass tops" and "grass roots" lobbying.

Some in our interfaith community did civil disobedience in the rotunda of the U.S. Capitol. My role was to be an observer in that action. I got to stand next to the capitol police as they got different instructions. The Democratic-controlled Senate wanted the interfaith group to be arrested and taken out the front door of the capitol where there was a rally against the Ryan budget going on. The Republican-controlled House did not want them to be arrested and wanted no attention drawn to them at all. Because the rotunda is in the center of the capitol, both sides of Congress control the territory. First the capitol police closed the rotunda to visitors so that they could arrest those praying. Then they got the message from the House and so they opened it up again. Back and forth it went. Our colleagues praying in the rotunda were on their knees so long on the marble floor that some of them had to sit down on the floor.

After about forty-five minutes of back and forth a compromise was reached: the faith leaders would be arrested, but they would be taken out through an inside elevator and into a parking garage.

Although civil disobedience drew some attention to the horrible budget, it did not really catch hold. So the interfaith community decided that we could not just be against the budget; rather, we should write a "Faithful" budget as an alternative to the Ryan budget. Late in December 2011 and then January 2012, our working groups scrambled to draft a budget that reflected the various positions of our coalition partners. It was tough going, and I thought that, even with a last-minute flurry of e-mails late into the night, we were going to lose the effort. I felt rather like Congress in the effort to make something good happen. But in the end, we were able to agree on a budget and put it forward as a responsible alternative to the irresponsible Ryan budget.

Little did we know then that this faithful alternative to the Ryan budget would become our best prop when we went on the road. That's because we didn't even know we were going on the road. Neither did we know we were being investigated by the Vatican for our work in passing health-care reform. When the world knew, we knew. And everything changed.

6

~

The Vatican Versus the Nuns

Passing health-care reform was a great and inspiring victory, resulting in a law that I trust—and I pray—will go down in American history as a landmark in our effort to achieve a more perfect union.

But as big as that moment was, the next morning we all woke up to the reality that the immediate economic crisis was still with us and demanded immediate attention. The unemployment rate was still stuck above 8 percent, which was absolutely untenable if the economy was to improve and it was absolutely intolerable as a matter of justice.

Many people were losing their jobs or at risk of losing their jobs except for the very wealthy, who were only getting richer. We knew this same anxiety at NETWORK as we had to lay off staff and not hire to fill vacancies. These were tough economic times. In fact, money was so tight for us at one point that I got a case of very

painful shingles as a result of my tension about money. We identified strongly with middle-class families who were slipping into
the working class, working-class families who were sliding into
poverty, and the poor who were falling off the scale—and off our
collective radar screen—altogether. Washington had to act, and
all the Republicans could focus on was angling to defeat President
Obama and the Democrats in 2012, and trying to cut spending
on programs that would support working Americans and their
families while cutting taxes for the wealthy. It was obscene, it
was unjust, and as history has shown, it wouldn't work. What was
needed was a stimulus, but the Republicans were going in another
direction.

The GOP plans, embodied in Wisconsin congressman Paul
Ryan's "Path to Prosperity" budget plan, would have done all sorts
of things besides giving most of the tax relief to the 1 percent and
cutting programs for the needy. The plan would also have eliminated income taxes on capital gains, dividends, and interest, and
it would have abolished the corporate income tax and the estate
tax while privatizing big chunks of Social Security and Medicare.
Among other things. The biggest irony is that it would not have
cut the deficit but would have increased it. Yet the Republican
talking points kept telling us that this was necessary because of
the deficit—a deficit that was created largely by Republican policies from the past decade. This latest hocus-pocus economics that
started circulating in 2011 didn't make sense fiscally, but it was
also not good for government or the needs of the most vulnerable
in our society. In promoting the plan early on, Congressman Ryan
said that Ayn Rand, the guru of bootstrap libertarians and author
of terrible novels that are like sacred texts to Representative Ryan
and his friends, was the inspiration for his policies. A year later,
perhaps with an eye to his political future, he claimed that Catholic social teachings informed these same views.

The former explanation seemed true; the latter did not. But

neither added up. Not that you could explain that to conservative Republicans. I went on Mike Huckabee's radio show shortly after it premiered in the spring of 2012 and he started going on about how one of the main reasons people are in poverty is because of the breakdown of the family, so we should do things to support marriage and the family.

Obviously the former Republican presidential candidate—and Baptist pastor—had not been briefed about who I was, and he didn't know much about Catholic social teaching.

"You are absolutely right," I told him. "And I practiced family law for eighteen years and I know that one of the biggest drivers behind the breakdown of the family is economic hardship and we need to raise the minimum wage so that low-income workers can in fact support their families."

Well, that totally flummoxed poor Mr. Huckabee, who couldn't understand how I could agree with him but have a different solution—and one that made economic sense.

Of course the issue was wages! The fact is that even people who are working full-time can still be in poverty. Many of these workers make enough to put a roof over their family's heads but not enough to put food on the table. In the United States, the "richest nation on earth," as we like to say, 20 percent of the population is living on $20,000 a year or less.[22] If the minimum wage were to have the same buying power today that it had in 1970, it would have to be about $10.49 an hour. If minimum wage had kept pace with productivity it would be $18.72 per hour.[23] In 2012, it was just $7.25 an hour.

Bishop Stephen E. Blaire, the chairman of the U.S. Conference of Catholic Bishops's Committee on Domestic Justice and Human Development, laid out the case in testimony before Congress in June of 2013 at a hearing dedicated to the seventy-fifth anniversary of the Fair Labor Standards Act, which codified the national minimum wage for the first time:

"We can begin the process of fixing our economy by returning the worker to the center of economic life," Blaire said. "One of the best ways to do that is with decent jobs that pay just wages, thereby honoring human dignity and restoring hope to workers and families. Increasing the minimum wage to a level that reflects the real economic reality faced by families today would go far in building an economy worthy of the humans that operate in it."

He cited data from the Working Poor Families Project showing that there were 10.4 million low-income working families in the United States in 2011, including 23.5 million children. "Work should be a ladder out of poverty for families, it should not trap them in poverty," the bishop said. "Yet this is where we find ourselves—a growing number of families are working but do not make enough to live in dignity. It is a scandal that the richest country in the world has allowed over 23 million children in working poor families to become the norm."

"A just wage confirms the dignity of the worker," he said. "And conversely, a wage that does not even allow a worker to support a family or meet basic human needs tears her down and demeans her dignity. The worker becomes just another commodity."

And it's not like the bishop is a left-wing propagandist pulling this policy out of thin air: in his testimony he cited Catholic teaching from Popes Leo XIII, John Paul II, Benedict XVI, and Francis, on the rights and dignity of workers.

And Bishop Blaire cited statistics from the Congressional Budget Office, which in 2012 reported that the average income of the wealthiest 1 percent of Americans had increased 275 percent over the past thirty years. The income of the poorest 20 percent, on average, increased by less than 20 percent, despite a dramatic increase in worker productivity over the same time.[24]

When I talk to groups, I like to use the human bar graph to illustrate the growth of income inequality. That's the exercise where you have audience members pace off a step for each 5 percent of income growth by the five sets of different income levels in the population. If you do it between the years 1979 and 2009, the distance, actual physical distance, between the top earners and those at the bottom—who are actually taking steps backward—is astonishing. It makes you realize why Mitt Romney could talk so dismissively about the 47 percent—because he couldn't even see them from where he is in the economy. He is so far away from the reality of hardworking, struggling families that he cannot know or imagine their true situation.

When I used the human bar graph at an event in New Jersey, at a college, a young man raised his hand and told us that he had suddenly realized that his family was in the lower 20 percent. "I never knew how hard my parents must have struggled until this moment," he said. Tears started down his face. "My parents protected us from all that worry. They have given us gifts I never knew. They got my sister and I to college! I am so grateful."

What can you do with that painful realization? Except embrace it, and embrace him and everyone like him. And work for change.

That's what we were determined to do, but it was hard to know how to make our voice heard amid the din of the campaigns that were filling the air in those intensely partisan days. We were also preparing to mark the fortieth anniversary of NETWORK's founding, in 1972, and we wanted to use that as an opportunity for mission, to get our message out. But we were struggling mightily to figure out how to do that.

On April 14, 2012, we hosted a grand party to celebrate the forty years since we opened our doors in Washington. We had a great panel that savored the achievements of the past by looking at policy issues through the lens of theological reflection and storytelling. Afterward we broke up into table discussions and again, the question that emerged from every group was: "This is terrific. But how to do we get our message out? How do we let more people know about our work on Capitol Hill? How do we spread the news?"

Four days later, on April 18, 2012, the Vatican answered those questions, and our prayers.

That's the day that Rome announced the results of the investigation of the umbrella organization representing most of the leaders of the nation's more than fifty thousand Catholic sisters. The group is called the Leadership Conference of Women Religious, or LCWR. The LCWR was formed in 1956 at the request of Pope Pius XII. It is a way to coordinate many of the activities of the myriad women's orders in America, and under canon law it answers to the Vatican. I was a member of LCWR when I was the leader of my community and now at NETWORK I am an associate member; that is, a participant but nonvoting member. Through this organization (and others like it in each country and/or region of the world) women and men religious coordinate their work and are free to speak their minds on issues of great moral and spiritual urgency in the church and in the world—and we often do.

And that, it seems, was the problem. The eight-page statement came from the Vatican's Congregation for the Doctrine of the Faith, which was called the Holy Office of the Inquisition until the 1960s. Under Pope John Paul II, the CDF was led for more than two decades by Cardinal Joseph Ratzinger—known to the world since 2005 as Pope Benedict XVI, John Paul's successor. The CDF charged the LCWR and, by extension, American nuns, with a whole host of sins against the hierarchy's delicate sensibilities.

For starters, we allegedly made public statements that "disagree with or challenge the bishops, who are the church's authentic teachers of faith and morals," and on top of that our regular conferences featured "a prevalence of certain radical feminist themes incompatible with the Catholic faith." Still worse: "(W)hile there has been a great deal of work on the part of LCWR promoting issues of social justice in harmony with the church's social doctrine, it is silent on the right to life from conception to natural death."

Moreover, the letter specifically cited our organization, NET-WORK, as being complicit in these alleged sins, especially focusing too much on the social justice mission of the Church—which is, if they had checked, what our mission has been doing for forty years. That was by design, and often in concert with the bishops and other Church leaders.

The Vatican further said that it had named Archbishop J. Peter Sartain of Seattle and two other bishops—Thomas J. Paprocki of Springfield, Illinois, and Leonard Blair of Toledo, Ohio (now in Hartford, Connecticut)—to lead the "reform" of the LCWR, a process that was to be completed within five years.

This was shocking—NETWORK had been folded into the two-year investigation into LCWR and had never been notified! LCWR leaders had been in talks with the Vatican investigators about the concerns over LCWR, but they also had no suspicion this was coming. The sweeping condemnation came like a bolt from the blue—it even took the American bishops by surprise—and it came without the courtesy of input or a response from our organization. The Vatican report gave a cursory nod to how the LCWR refuted the charges and then dismissed the rebuttals as "inadequate." There was absolutely no conversation with NET-WORK. We couldn't even speak for ourselves.

The day the report dropped I was up in the Finger Lakes region of New York State and had just finished giving a workshop—you can't make this up—to local LCWR members on "How to talk to people who think differently."

The first inkling I had that NETWORK was on the Vatican radar was when I got a call on my cell phone from our communications director, Stephanie Niedringhaus. I had been on Current TV the night before with former Michigan governor Jennifer

Granholm talking about the U.S. bishops' statement that said that Paul Ryan's budget—which Ryan now claimed to be inspired by his Catholic faith—failed basic "moral criteria" of protecting the poor and vulnerable.

I was sure Stephanie was calling about that, because it was the biggest story around.

"Uh. No, Simone," she said. "We've been mentioned by the *Vatican.*"

"WHAT!" I almost yelled into the phone.

I mean, what else was there to say? At the very moment we were standing shoulder to shoulder with the bishops in their fight to protect the poor and advance the social justice mission of the Church, the Vatican criticized us for focusing too much on protecting the poor and advancing the social justice mission of the Church.

I knew that the LCWR leaders couldn't say much of anything publicly because of the excruciatingly difficult position they were in. NETWORK, however, was independent of direct Vatican ties. So as I absorbed this shocking news, I also tried to think strategically. I knew that I could respond to the press, whereas the LCWR leaders, who were still in Rome on their annual visit, had a much more difficult task ahead. So I wound up fielding a lot of media calls in those first few hours, walking in circles around a dusty parking lot next to a lovely lake in upstate New York.

Why did this happen? What was going on behind the scenes?

There are many aspects to the answer, but what the LCWR investigation really highlighted was the wide and, sadly, growing gulf between the way religious communities live the Gospel and the way the clerical culture—mainly the bishops—want to run the Church.

It was principally about politics, not faith. For example, I knew right off that NETWORK had been included in the censure for one main reason: health-care reform. We were one of the main reasons health-care reform was passed, and some of the bishops would neither forgive nor forget—even though it's been shown they were wrong in their objections. The Catholic bishops had received very bad political advice from those claiming that there was federal funding of abortion in the bill. And then they blamed us because we disagreed with that erroneous assessment.

One of the sisters who signed our health-care letter described it this way: the girls' team played the boys' team and for once the girls' team won. And the boys are angry. Just look at the timing: the Vatican appointed Bishop Leonard Blair to carry out a doctrinal assessment of LCWR in April 2008 and he submitted his report to the Vatican in June 2010, little more than three months after the health-care law was signed by President Obama—with me looking on proudly, and in front of the camera.

The fact that Cardinal William Levada, former archbishop of San Francisco, was head of the CDF at the time was also part of the dynamic in that he is an American and he brought his American focus with him to the job. (Cardinal Ratzinger, who had moved up the ladder to become Pope Benedict XVI in 2005, named Levada as his replacement.)

One such preoccupation was the growing—and profoundly unfortunate—divergence between Catholics focused on issues of sexual morality and those called to work for social justice. The concerns are different to a great degree, yes. But they overlap and should buttress each other, or at least not be in conflict. The Catholic Church has a "consistent ethic of life" outlook that sees everyone and everything as worthy of protection and concern, from the baby in the womb to the single mother to the inmate on death row and, yes, even the financier on Wall Street. This "seamless garment" was most famously propounded by the late Chicago cardinal Joseph Bernardin, who was also attacked by conservatives (many of them his fellow churchmen) for his view.

Yet abortion rights have come to dominate the institutional Catholic Church's priorities, creating an opportunity for champions of one segment of the Church's ministry to downplay the social justice agenda. The Church's mission has thus become a competition rather than a model of complementarity, and the hierarchy has increasingly put its thumb on the scale to the advantage of what I tend to call the "pro-birth" movement rather than the "pro-life" movement. That division works to the detriment of the entire Body of Christ.

I don't think abortion is a good choice. I think it is a hard, difficult, and often devastating decision for women. I've actually never found anybody who was pro-death. We only add to the pain of the situation when we make it into an abstract fight about principles rather than an effort to support people. I came to understand some of the anguish of these situations when I was practicing family law and I was appointed to represent a thirteen-year-old girl who had been raped and impregnated by her uncle. She ended up having a miscarriage. From that episode I gained some insight into the horrible, agonizing choice that was facing this terrified girl and others like her.

Yet the very phrase "pro-life" has too often meant "harsh and exclusionary," and associating myself with such a movement made me judgmental and giving a witness that was contrary to the Gospel call. Not to mention that such tactics turned off the very public we are supposed to convince! The extremism of the Right has done much to alienate people from what I think is the faithful response to political questions. It has taken real, concerted effort for me to reclaim that pro-life language. I always try to speak of life beyond birth so that all people know that faith values more than just the blessed arrival of a baby into this world.

In my view, a central problem is that the fight over abortion has been about the political consequences of being pro-life rather than focusing on reducing the actual abortion rate. I'm pro-life, but I'm not pro-criminalization of abortion. I think we should nourish women and take care of them and support them and do what's necessary so they can make that choice for life. But I don't think we should criminalize them. Poverty is the great driver of the abortion rate. In recent decades—even during the Obama administration—the abortion rate for everybody above the lowest 20 percent in income has gone down. For women in poverty, it has gone up. The numbers are clear: It's about economics!

But the Vatican censure of the LCWR was also the latest example of the hierarchy's long-standing discomfort with what women religious have been doing in the nearly fifty years since the Second Vatican Council ended. As I said earlier, we women religious—we sisters and nuns—took Vatican II's call to return to the roots of our vocation in a radical way. "Radical feminists"? Yes, in a sense we are.

We struggled to discover what our calling was, how to embody the Gospel in a radical way. We had big fights. We came to new insights. Yet that is exactly what our world is hungry for. People in the United States have responded warmly to the work of sisters, and the bishops mistook that honor for the sisters thinking that they were in charge of the Church's teaching. No sister I know thinks she has the responsibility for the institution of the Church. Rather we walk with people in everyday life and try to live the Gospel in that context. This living reality gives us hearts of compassion for the struggle of our world. We strive to be faithful to Jesus's call to love everyone. It appears that people find this attractive and describe it as spiritual leadership. The bishops, on the other hand, take their role as chiefly one of protecting the institution. They live by rules and regulations that many people experience as judgmental and off-putting. It seems to me that some bishops are angry that the sisters are given a respect that the bishops think they alone deserve. As often happens, the effort to protect the institution at all costs winds up backfiring. Hence this sad situation in which we find ourselves—bishops protecting pedophile priests and other abusers and the entire Church paying the wages of those sins.

Any Catholic has to be suffering at this moment given all the scandals and divisions in the Church. It is terribly hard, terribly sad. Some have asked me why don't I leave the Church. But that is impossible. For me, the spiritual journey is the deepest piece of me, and my faith tradition brought me the skills and grace for this spiritual, contemplative pilgrimage. So how can I turn my back on the foundation of my being? The institutional Catholic Church is so much more than the leadership.

Radical faith in action is not about taking away something that is "theirs" and giving it to someone else. The "heresy" of ordaining women to the priesthood is the best example of this false way of thinking. The bishops say ordination is for them, and the women and girls can't have it. But I think we might be making a mistake in focusing all our arguments on the stance of the bishops. Perhaps there is a larger vision of priesthood that needs to be considered. Think of baptism: we have baptism of the "ordinary" kind, by water and performed by an ordained minister. Yet in urgent circumstances a Catholic can baptize another person. And we also have baptism by blood, which is martyrdom. There is also "baptism by desire," the presumption of a sacramental seal of those who earnestly desire to be part of the body but have no way to formally join, or are otherwise impeded from joining. Or take the Eucharist, the "summit and source" of the Catholic life. Yes, Christ becomes truly present in a real way in the bread and wine. But as the Second Vatican Council stressed, Jesus is also present in the people assembled there, and in the word proclaimed, as well as in the celebrants of the sacrament.

For many sisters and others in the Church, the problem with priestly ordination is that the Church has only acknowledged the most common clerical form of ordination as opposed to other

forms of ordination that occur. We need to live into the alternatives. For instance, when I was head of our community, it finally
became clear to me that I was called at that moment to be priestly
to my sisters—to preside at prayer, to break bread in a variety of
ways: to share their lives, to forgive, to anoint. In very sacred
ways, that was a priestly service for a time. It is not male bishop-
ordained priesthood. It's not parochial, not part of a parish and
ecclesial structure. But I was in a sense ordained for that time for
my sisters.

This entails a reenvisioning of the idea of ordination, not
so much changing the existing one. The problem is that we get
caught in a fight about the traditional view that serves to reinforce
that standard approach.

Yes, perhaps I am hopelessly naive, even more so about the
Church perhaps than I am about politics. I also keep expecting
the Church to be Christian, and yes, it would be nice if the bishops practiced what they preached. The fact is that any organization that took 350 years to figure out that Galileo might be right
is not noted for rapid change. The challenge that we face in the
Roman Catholic Church is not so much a problem of faith but a
problem of culture. What we sisters are doing is the enculturating
of faith into democratic culture. In a democratic culture we know
that diverse views lead to insight and deeper understandings.
This is a good thing. The problem is that the existing culture of
the institutional Catholic Church is monarchical, and monarchs
are threatened when the people speak up, when the people take
the initiative. Traditionally, monarchs never voluntarily give up
power. So I don't know how this will work out.

In the meantime, however, the leadership sure can create difficulties for those of us in religious life. In announcing their plan
to "reform" the LCWR, the Vatican claimed that because so many
people are following us we are therefore usurping the roles of the

bishops as teachers in the Church. But we're not. We're living our lives by living the Gospel and doing the ministry of our communities. The church hierarchy has all the authority—though maybe not the power—they think, or want.

Part of the problem is that some of the bishops have lost sight of what spiritual leadership is. Many of the bishops are so frightened because they know they're supposed to be spiritual leaders but they don't know what that is. So they think enforcing the rules is what it's all about. It's not. My hunch is that they are focused on false dichotomies: fear versus joy; exclusion versus inclusion; rules versus the gospel story. The second option in all of those— joy, inclusion, Gospel—will win every time.

As Pope Francis has said, the biblical parable speaks about the good shepherd who leaves his 99 sheep to find the one that is lost. "Today," the pope said, "we have one in the pen and 99 we need to go looking for." And we must do everything to reach them, to be with them:

> A church that limits itself to just carrying out administrative duties, caring for its tiny flock, is a church that in the long run will get sick. The pastor who isolates himself is not a true pastor of sheep, but a "hairdresser" for sheep who spends his time putting curlers on them instead of going to look for others.[25]

At every turn, Francis has emphasized the needs of the poor, the imperative to go out to the margins, to stand with the people, to work with others—believers, nonbelievers, whoever—for the common good. He has blasted the clericalism of the institutional Catholic Church, the "peacocks" in the hierarchy who strut about in their ecclesiastical finery, and the "careerism" and "ambition" (his words, not mine) of too many priests and bishops. The Church today must embrace simplicity and humility and must "prune away" all the needless overgrowth that is choking our message and mission.

"A Christian, if he is not a revolutionary, in this time, he is not a Christian!" he told the convention of the Diocese of Rome. Amen!

Just as important, in his landmark interview that was published in several Jesuit magazines in September 2013, Francis framed the teachings of the Church in almost the exact same terms that prompted the crackdown on the American sisters. He lamented that the Church seems "obsessed" by a few teachings to the exclusion of crucial other tenets, and he called for a "new balance" in our stance toward the world:

We cannot insist only on issues related to abortion, gay marriage and the use of contraceptive methods. This is not possible. I have not spoken much about these things, and I was reprimanded for that. But when we speak about these issues, we have to talk about them in a context. The teaching of the church, for that matter, is clear and I am a son of the church, but it is not necessary to talk about these issues all the time.[26]

Lucky for Francis, he is the pope and unlikely to be investigated by his own doctrinal officials. How this will play out with the LCWR and NETWORK and the American sisters, on the other hand, I don't know. Many of us were taken aback when a Vatican communiqué in April of 2013, a month after Francis was elected, announced that the head of the CDF, Cardinal Gerhard Ludwig Müller—who had replaced Cardinal Levada a few months before—met with LCWR leaders and told them that he had recently discussed the Vatican report with the pope, "who reaffirmed the findings of the Assessment and the program of reform."[27]

But in June, in a long and informal meeting with the leadership of religious orders in Latin America, the pope took a more casual approach to the LCWR investigation, and toward curial directives in general:

> Say you err, make a blunder—it happens! Maybe you'll re-
> ceive a letter from the Congregation for Doctrine, say-
> ing that they were told this or that thing . . . But don't let
> it bother you. Explain what you have to explain, but keep
> going forward . . . Open doors, do something where life is
> calling out.[28]

That sounded more like Pope Francis's expected answer to institutional preoccupations. He has been saying that he wants bishops to be pastors rather than branch managers, but he also needs time to appoint good bishops and he needs a talent pool to draw from. That's a challenge. Then again the Holy Spirit is always working to convert us to ways of love. Everyone of us is a work in process, including bishops and sisters.

All this makes me hopeful that Francis will begin the neces-sary process of change—of revolution. The fact that he is a Jesuit is a good start. The Society of Jesus embraced Vatican II's call of reform and the "preferential option for the poor" with as much enthusiasm and profound commitment as so many communities of women religious—even unto death in many tragic cases. But just as important is the pope's grounding in the contemplative tradition. The spirituality of St. Ignatius Loyola, founder of the Jesuits, is powerful and bracing, and the problem with most of the Church's leadership has been that the bishops have no training in contemplative practices.

Contemplative practice has been a source of joy and hope through this whole LCWR episode and the resulting Nuns on the Bus phenomenon. By staying anchored in the reality of God alive in our midst, we at NETWORK and other sisters have found the ways to walk faithfully even when we disagree with Vatican action. We can be clearly who we are called to be, but we do not have to be adversarial. We can attempt to stay open and loving to those who criticize us. This is not easy, but it is the Gospel way.

We saw that in St. Louis in August of 2012, when the LCWR held its annual meeting, the first after the Vatican censure had been announced. The intervening months had been tough ones for the bishops and for Rome; both got hammered in the court of public opinion as people who knew the sisters as the embodiment of the Gospel in the Catholic Church in the United States rallied to our side. The *sensus fidelium*, as they call it, the sense of the faithful, saw that Vatican power play for what it is, I think, and we sisters—led by the estimable Sister Pat Farrell and the rest of the leadership team—were so wise and intentional about responding not in kind but in charity and with firmness. Pat and so many others had experience in Central America in the 1980s dealing with Latin American dictators and gun-toting soldiers that a few bishops and curial bureaucrats were not likely to make them cower in fear or lash out in a panic. The gift of their historical learning was a treasure for finding a faithful and loving way through the crisis.

Nonviolent resistance can carry the day and convey the Gospel message, and that is what the women of LCWR tried to do—some nine hundred of us gathered for several days of dialogue and prayer and discernment. And at the end, LCWR opted to keep the channels of communication open, committing to dialogue but always insisting on the integrity of our mission, based on the words of Jesus.[29]

"There is an inherent existential tension between the complementary roles of hierarchy and religious (the nuns) which is not likely to change," Sister Farrell told us in her farewell address as president of LCWR. "In an ideal ecclesial world, the different roles are held in creative tension, with mutual respect and appreciation, in an environment of open dialogue, for the building up of the whole Church."

Pat spoke of the nuns' public "struggle to balance our life on the periphery with fidelity to the center."

Sister Farrell also spoke of how the sisters have historically been committed to serving the poor and marginalized as well as to pushing boundaries within the Church. That sometimes led to suppression by the hierarchy, she said, but also to sainthood for many nuns, and to far-reaching changes that have benefited Catholics as a whole.

Pat invoked an array of images to describe the role of religious communities in the past and in more recent time, including one of my favorites—that of the lightning rod that "draws the charge to itself, channels and grounds it, providing protection."

The reality is that we do what we do for others and for the Church, not for ourselves. Many say that our way of life—women religious, the nuns and sisters—is dying. But we have always responded to what the Church needed, where the Church—that is, the People of God—was going. In the 1940s and 1950s, there was an explosion of vocations because the People of God needed the workforce, and we got it. So we all took that as normative. But then the needs changed.

My theory is that if we stop focusing on what we used to have or what we used to need, but focus rather on what we are being given, maybe then we would better know the needs that we are supposed to be responding to.

Here is where we women religious are: We are getting old. We can't do what we used to do, but we strive to live from our spiritual center. But we can listen. We've got the hunger for deep truth. We have the capacity to live in community. And we are being forced to wrestle with death and dying, because our friends are dying,

Now look at what the needs of our country are: a hunger for

spirituality; a hunger for somebody to listen; a deep, deep, deep need for community. And Lord knows we need some way to talk realistically and with faith about death and dying. So when I look at the gifts we are being given and at the needs of our country, I think we need to wake up as women religious to find a way to welcome people in, to share this richness of what we have. That is the challenge, the invitation, the opportunity. It's all trusting that we are one body—that God is with us every moment, that we will not be orphaned. But we have to respond to the nudge.

And we have to keep opening out to the needs of our time. In a brief talk to the other cardinals before the conclave, Cardinal Jorge Mario Bergoglio decried the ecclesiastical narcissism of a "self-referential" Church. That four-minute address probably got him elected Pope Francis. I hope so. Because I don't want to be distracted by a fight with the Church. Our mission is bigger than that. This hunger transcends the Catholic Church. But I rejoice that the Spirit is using this struggle with the institutional Church to promote the bigger need of addressing the issue of poverty in our nation. If the Vatican had never censured us, there would never have been a bus trip. We must stay focused on the bigger concern as Pope Francis says.

"I prefer a church that messes up for doing something than one that's sick for remaining closed inside itself," Francis said after he was elected pope.

We cannot remain closed in on ourselves—Catholics and non-Catholics alike. In the United States, in a pluralistic culture, it's about "we the people." But how were we at NETWORK, we Catholic sisters and lay staffers, going to do our part? As I looked ahead in 2012, that is what really worried me.

7

Road Trip

To be honest, after a few days of fielding calls and doing media appearances on the Vatican crackdown, I was getting bored—and frustrated. Catholic sisters by definition are not about having the spotlight on ourselves. We are all about the mission of our ministry. Here the bishops had given us this great gift of publicity for our mission, at the very moment we needed it most. The recession was dragging on, the people were suffering, and the regressive Paul Ryan budget was the talk of the Beltway. And we at NETWORK had a policy response to all those problems, plus a bigger platform than we had enjoyed in the past forty years of our existence.

But how could we capitalize on it? It seemed to me that we had too small of an imagination for this great moment.

As I was doing my daily meditation one morning following the hubbub over Rome's investigation, what came to me was that I

needed to ask for help. I didn't want to make this another internal
Church battle among Catholics. We have had enough of those, and
besides, the people we were hoping to help through our ministries aren't all Catholic, not by a long shot. And our allies in finding solutions and serving others aren't always Catholic either.

So the next thing that came to me was the image of the Samaritan woman at the well. In the story, told in the Gospel of John,
Jesus and his disciples are traveling through Samaria—a foreign
land—whose residents were not exactly on good terms with Jews
like Jesus. Jesus is tired from the journey, it is midday and it is
hot, and he is alone because the disciples have gone into town to
buy food. He is sitting by a well when a Samaritan woman comes
to draw water. He asks her for a drink though his people and her
people by custom did not associate with each other. "You are a Jew
and I am a Samaritan woman. How can you ask me for a drink?"
she says.

So here is Jesus in a strange land, not among his own, and
he's talking to an outcast. And not only talking to an outcast, but
he's asking the outcast for help. *Why shouldn't I follow that model?*
I thought.

My opportunity came at the next meeting of the Common
Purpose Project, a collection of progressive advocacy groups in
Washington. Every Tuesday evening when Congress is in session,
we have something called the Big Table when we get together to
talk about what we are doing on a policy level and to lobby the
White House staffers who also come to the meetings. Basically we
strategize and energize ourselves for the coming policy struggles.

At the next Big Table meeting after the Vatican censure, the
administration officials present reported on a variety of pend-
ing issues, including the budget. At the end of the meeting, the
subcommittee members working on the implementation of the
health-care law reported on their work. Then there was time
for announcements. I raised my hand and said, "Well, you may

have seen that I've been in the press lately." Everybody laughed. I plunged ahead, proceeding to tell them that we at NETWORK needed help figuring out how to respond to this opportunity. Then Ron Pollack, the head of Families USA, gave the most amazing tribute to what we at NETWORK had done to help pass health-care reform. When he was done, everyone in the room stood up and applauded. It was so touching, such a remarkable moment for me, for all of us. Immediately many of the participants pledged to help, and many came up to me and gave me their business cards. (That's how people interact in Washington, you see, even in the age of Facebook!)

So we set up a meeting at NETWORK's offices for May 14 to try to figure out what do we do next to advance our mission, how to take advantage of the unique chance we had been given.

It was in the course of that meeting that Nuns on the Bus was born. For me it was a sign of the Holy Spirit that in a city where people are quick to grab credit whenever they can, nobody remembers who first said: "Road trip." But by the end of the meeting it was clear that we were going on the road and we were going in a wrapped bus, because someone said that's what you do with these sorts of tours.

Luckily, Caren Benjamin from Americans United for Change knew all about this sort of thing, having organized the Bush Legacy bus tour. She connected us to the Markham Group, an events company that specializes in political campaign buses (they had done the Kerry presidential campaign bus, for example). The team at Markham got folks together to staff the bus, including Scott Pollard, who was brilliant in setting everything up and schooling me in the arcana of bus tours.

They were also very patient. On one of our first conference calls, Scott asked me how many sisters I expected and I said I thought thirty to forty sisters was reasonable. There was a long silence, and Scott's voice sounded as though he was going to have apoplexy at the thought of wrangling dozens of nuns. "There's only twelve seats," he finally said. What? I said I thought this was going to be a big bus. Twelve seats sounded like a van, no? No, he explained. In these big campaign buses there is only lounge seating, and room for a bathroom, a little kitchen area, storage, the works.

That's when he schooled us, ever so politely, on how these things worked.

So we had a bus, and then we got a logo and a slogan thanks to our designer, Gene Kim, who, as I mentioned earlier, assumed our casual tagline, "Nuns on the Bus," was the actual name.

The beautiful logo she created—"Nuns on the Bus: A drive for faith, family, and fairness"—was perfect.

Now our other concern about the design for the bus was that it should be positive, attractive, and uplifting, showing the dignity of people who serve and are served. "No pathetic images too often used in charity advertisements—images that exploit and under-mine the dignity of those portrayed," insisted Sister Marge Clark, one of our lobbyists. The entire staff quickly concurred. Hence the bright blue background and the smiling faces that adorned our bus.

Now, where would this bus go exactly? I did I have a rough map in my head that was anchored by key congressional districts where there were also motherhouses of women religious. We needed nuns, and we needed free places to stay. And we needed congressional representatives to lobby. So that map made sense, and we started fleshing out a detailed itinerary.

But I refused to go public until we had the money to fund the trip. This was going to be the biggest thing NETWORK had ever done, and I was really nervous about collecting the more than $200,000 that we would need, at minimum, to pull it off.

Oh, me of little faith! Just ten days after this idea was birthed, we had collected commitments to cover all the basic costs. It was like wildfire! Which I found an appropriate image since we were in June now and Pentecost was approaching. It was time to spread the word about the trip, but it was also time for me to head back to Los Angeles for our annual weekend celebration of Pentecost—the main feast of our Spirit-centered Sisters of Social Service.

Soon after our first planning meeting for the Nuns on the Bus trip, Sally Steenland from the Center for American Progress, who was at our first meeting, had gone to a big media event and dinner in Washington that the Catholic bishops put on to talk about how they were being persecuted by the Obama administration because of the insurance mandate to provide contraception coverage to women. The bishops explained that in order to counter this oppression, they needed to launch their own campaign, which they called the "Fortnight for Freedom." Personally, I think Nuns on the Bus was catchier, and our cause—social justice—was more obviously under siege. Religious freedom? Our bus tour was showing just how free we were in this country. Our people were the ones who were suffering from the injustice of poverty.

But the bishops had their project, and we had ours. Interestingly, their fortnight would coincide almost precisely with our tour. We had mapped out a route by this point, beginning in Iowa on June 18, 2012, and ending in Washington, D.C., on July 2. In between we would stop in Wisconsin, Illinois, Indiana, Michigan, Ohio, Pennsylvania, Maryland, and Virginia, winding up at the U.S. Capitol—a total of nine states in two weeks.

In any event, at the bishops' glitzy launch party, Sally was sitting next to Laurie Goodstein, the religion reporter for the *New York Times*, and she started telling Laurie about an amazing meeting she had attended the day before where we were discussing the possibility of doing a bus trip. Nuns, a bus, a multistate tour through recession-hit areas during the presidential campaign— Laurie's journalistic senses started to tingle and she said she wanted to know more. So Sally told me to call Laurie before she left Washington. I called her and she was very excited about the possibilities for the story and asked me if she could have an exclusive. I agreed, after realizing that a story in the New York Times was another gift of the Spirit, and Laurie started working on her piece. But I told her she could not run with it until we had the money committed and some logistics set up. There was no way we were going to jump the gun until we were sure we could pull this thing off.

When I got back from my community's Pentecost celebration a few days later, Laurie was calling and asking me please, please to let her run the story. She was afraid someone else would get it, which was understandable. Hey, an exclusive in the New York Times? That's not such a bad way to get some buzz going.

The story ran on Wednesday, June 6, with the headline: "Nuns, Rebuked by Rome, Plan Road Trip to Spotlight Social Issues."

It opened:

In a spirited retort to the Vatican, a group of Roman Catholic nuns is planning a bus trip across nine states this month, stopping at homeless shelters, food pantries, schools and health care facilities run by nuns to highlight their work with the nation's poor and disenfranchised.

The bus tour is a response to a blistering critique of American nuns released in April by the Vatican's doctrinal office, which included the accusation that the nuns are outspoken on issues of social justice, but silent on other issues the church considers crucial: abortion and gay marriage.

The sisters plan to use the tour also to protest cuts in programs for the poor and working families in the federal budget that was passed by the House of Representatives and proposed by Representative Paul D. Ryan, a Wisconsin Republican who cited his Catholic faith to justify the cuts.

"We're doing this because these are life issues," said Sister Simone Campbell, executive director of Network, a liberal social justice lobby in Washington. "And by lifting up the work of Catholic sisters, we will demonstrate the very programs and services that will be decimated by the House budget."[30]

Buzz we got, and fast. Requests for newspaper interviews and television appearances came rolling in.

Among the offers spawned by the wave of attention was one from the owner of the Fort Des Moines Hotel whose reservation manager called to say that the owner wanted to give the sisters free rooms for the night that we were to be in town. I said that was very sweet of him and I would get back to him. I knew that we were going to Ames, not Des Moines. But when we started making travel plans to get to the beginning of the trip in Iowa, I learned we had to go through Des Moines to get to Ames. I called back immediately to accept the gracious offer. Still, our plan was just to arrive in Des Moines the night before and, in the morning, hop on the bus and head to Ames.

The Sisters of Humility of Mary in Des Moines had other ideas. "Wait," they said, "you can't do that. We have to bless you!" So they set up a lovely Sunday evening prayer service at Holy Trinity Parish with the great pastor there, Father Mike Amadeo. That's when I started to get a sense of what the Holy Spirit had in store for us. They had people at the airport with signs to welcome us, they had a caravan from the airport to accompany us, and then they had this incredibly moving vigil that first night, June 17.

More than three hundred people showed. Some drove all the way from Omaha, others from Sioux City. The pulpit had a banner that read "Courage in Struggle," and when my turn to speak came I really felt the Spirit moving. They videotaped what I said and put it right up on the Internet. That was the beginning of en-Spirited wildness. I told the assembly:[31]

> You cannot control what is happening. We cannot do it. But where our passion really gets generated is in what we can control in our electoral process. What we can control is what they are doing in Congress.
>
> The reason we are out around the country is because most people don't know what the House of Representatives has just done. They've already done this; they passed Paul Ryan's proposed budget without any change! . . . (H)e likes to claim he's going to decrease the debt but the CBO (Congressional Budget Office) says he's actually going to increase the debt. Well, that doesn't sound good. And not only is he going to increase the debt but he's going to do that by giving further tax cuts to the top two percent under the guise that those are the folks who create jobs.
>
> Now, I don't want to say anything, but those are the very same folks who have had a significant tax cut for ten years, and I have yet to see a job. And not only have I yet to see a job, but I have yet to see significant salary increases for those who work so hard, day in and day out.

We were rolling now, and the people were inspired, and inspiring.

I talked about the explosion in CEO compensation—"It's shocking that CEOs would get an increase when the very people who create their wealth don't"—and spoke about Paul Ryan claiming that his policies reflect Catholic social teaching. "Catholic social teaching! If he had never uttered those words, I don't think we would have had a bus trip," I told them. "He made me mad. And I'm a stubborn woman . . ."

I even cited Pope Benedict XVI in his encyclical *Charity in*

Truth. Yes, it's a bit tedious to read—it's a papal encyclical after all. But there are some great points in there, especially for those who want to cite church teaching to show Paul Ryan how wrong he is. Benedict says clearly in there that you can only have individual responsibility as a keystone of your community if you have intense solidarity. "If we are one in our spirit of community, if we know what each other needs, if we know and respond to the needs of the community, then we can have individual responsibility," I told them.

"Our solidarity is what will keep us from slipping into isolation, loneliness, and depression. Because the only time we are fully human is when we are fully connected with each other."

Paul Ryan's budget wasn't going to connect us; it was going to disconnect us, I said. It was going to cut food stamps that help the working poor, and that also help businesses—alas—because food stamps allow low-wage workers to feed their families so they can continue working that low-wage job. You're welcome, Business Community!

The cuts the Republicans wanted to make were so severe that for charities to make up the shortfall in the cuts to food stamps alone—which is what some suggested—every church, synagogue, mosque, and house of worship in the United States would have had to raise an extra $50,000 a year for ten years. The Ryan budget would have cut two thousand kids from the Head Start program in Iowa alone and would have meant a loss of one thousand jobs.

This is wrong. This is not our country. This is not "We the people." This is not the Constitution based on the idea that all are created equal . . . That's who we are. We need to invest in the future. We have benefited so much from what our parents and grandparents did for us. What are we leaving our kids and grandkids?

I concluded by talking about the images that had surfaced in prayer during this time:

The first image that came to me was the burning bush: Yahweh calls out to Moses, "Come, take off your shoes, this is sacred ground." And what God says to Moses is, "I have heard the cry of my people. My people are enslaved and without hope. I have heard their cry."

And he sends Moses to set them free. And I had this image that we are called to be this bush, where God can flame up in our lives, and we can set our people free. It's the work of God in us that can make the difference. It's God flaming up and giving light—and a little bit of destruction . . . But if we are faithful to God we will not be destroyed. We will be enlivened.

And look tonight! Look at this life that is being generated! Together we can be the burning bush! Together we can let God shine in our midst!

I continued:

Two days ago, the image that came to me in prayer was the story of Ezekiel and the dry bones. Remember that story? Ezekiel walks in the valley of dry bones—it's pretty grim. Then God says, "Prophesy, that these bones can rise." And then they get sinew on them, and they get skin, and they kind of look human. But they have no breath, and they have no hope. And what God says is: "Prophesy and breathe on them." And the breath of the spirit gives them life and hope.

And the powerful thing I'm discovering by this bizarro bus trip—the foolishness for Christ's sake—is that it gives breath, it gives hope, and laughter. You know Dante says that laughter is the language of angels.

And so my friends we have serious work ahead. We cannot do this alone. But we have each other, and we have each other's backs. If we are the bush that can let God flame up out of control and go to nine states—and try to stay sane in the process—if we are free to let God be in our lives, if we are free to breathe on each other and bring out this hope, something new IS going to come. I have no idea what it is. I had no idea we'd be here two weeks ago. But here we are.

Who's willing to be part of this community to move this forward? Can you support each other? Can you breathe on each other? Can you give each other hope? Because I want you to know one thing: your presence here tonight, your breath here tonight breathes on us, and gives us hope. So we will have the stamina, the courage to keep going. Because we have solidarity with the folks here in Des Moines and in all the other places we are headed, I bet we find the same.

And if we have solidarity, then we can each take responsibility to form that more perfect union. Right? Right! And let the people say, AMEN!

"Amen!" they responded as one, and after the blessing at the end, people came up and started telling us their stories and where they had come from, and what this all meant to them. Some even started stuffing money in our pockets, which was not *our* intention at all! What touched me as much as anything was the range of people there. Those attending were not just Catholics; they were Lutherans and the Unitarians and Presbyterians and Methodists. They were Jews and Buddhists—who knew that Des Moines has a Buddhist community? Others said, "I'm not religious but I really like what you say." That happened so often during the next two weeks. "I'm not religious but I love your message," someone said to me. "It's your day job I don't understand!"

That was part of the mystery of it all, and it only deepened and grew richer.

Those of us going on the bus got together for prayer the next morning, Monday, and then a whole bunch of people came to see us off. They brought balloons and flowers. We were all just sort of stunned.

We started off with five nuns because I only had seven seats on the bus that I could offer to the sisters and I had to give two to media since the press interest was so high. Some sisters would come for part of the tour, and one drove a chase car the first leg. We made the back part of the bus a "cloister," as we dubbed it, so the sisters could hide from the reporters, who rode up front.

Television reporters from CBS, CNN, ABC, and Al Jazeera were in tow plus a bunch of print journalists from all over as we set off for Ames in a small caravan.

Our driver for the trip was a wonderful guy named Bill Kann. He was also the driver on Elvis's last tour, which we hoped wasn't an omen of some sort. But it was pretty cool for us. We kept trying to get stories out of him, but he wouldn't bite. "I'm not talking about your trip so I'm not going to talk about Elvis."

What happens on the bus, stays on the bus. I had to respect that.

Our goal on the bus trip was to do four things every day: to lift up the work that sisters do by visiting the ministries they operate; to lobby local politicians to vote against the Ryan budget and for our Faithful budget plan; to do media events; and in the evening to hold what we called "friend-raisers," a riff on the politico's usual campaign trail fund-raiser. At our friend-raisers we would meet supporters and share stories more informally and reenergize for the next day's events.

That was the plan. But it took a few days to get into our rhythm, that's for sure. As we started out, we didn't have a finalized itinerary beyond the first week, and our staff back in Washington was scrambling to put the rest of the trip together even as we set out. We were traveling on a prayer, maybe the best way to go.

On that first day, our first destination was the new Ames field office of a prominent tea party Republican—and a Catholic—Rep. Steve King, who had voted for the Ryan budget. We had scheduled an appointment with a staffer, but when we showed up, media in tow, there was a neatly typed note taped to the glass door: "Out in the field with constituents. Not available."[31]

It was hot, even for Iowa in June, yet more than a hundred supporters had showed up at King's office to welcome us. It was an amazing sight. And yes, great publicity—for us, if not for Representative King.

That's how the Holy Spirit works sometimes. The story was not the meeting, as we expected, but the snub. And the photo, worth more than a thousand words, was of me trying to slip a copy of the Faithful budget under their door, with our message. If the staffers had just been there and met with us, it would have been nothing. But instead it was an explosion.

I made a few remarks outside the office about the devastating impact of the Ryan budget, and about our counterproposal, and mostly about our vision for a united America where people would talk to one another about our common problems rather than running away from each other.

"In Washington, D.C., it's really easy for congresspeople to hide from other points of view," I said. "It's all about bringing people together and about solving the problems of our nation. We can't afford to hide from each other. This . . . breaks my heart. Our nation is better than this."

After that we headed to a newly opened Salvation Army store in Ames, and there was an even larger crowd, hundreds of well-wishers and local and national press.

I talked some more about the Ryan budget, and then Jodi

O'Donnell, who had been asked by the Take Down Steve King campaign to speak on our behalf, gave a brief, powerful commentary about solidarity for the poor.

"I once was a Catholic but gave it up," she said. "However, I have never given up the Catholic social justice teachings it promotes, and I feel honored to be here with Sister Simone. . . . America is not in decline from the people at the bottom who game the system, but from those at the top who do."

The crowd was terrific, staying and supporting us despite increasingly brutal heat.

"I came here to stand up for justice and helping the poor," the Reverend Donna Ewert, a United Church of Christ pastor from Harlan, told *National Catholic Reporter*, which was covering the event. "They are the ones getting the raw end of the deal and falling through the gaps. And the churches are supposed to fill the gaps? They are depleted, too."

"It's a Jesus thing," said the Reverend Joy Gonnerman, an Evangelical Lutheran Church in America pastor from Kimballton. "I saw Sister Simone and loved what she said. This is all about showing solidarity with the Gospel and speaking truth to power. This endless voice of law bothers me."

Best of all was the little girl, maybe seven or eight years old, who showed up outside Representative King's office with her little stuffed tiger. She said her name was Ophelia. So I remarked that she had a really big name and wondered what her friends call her. "They call me Little O," she said helpfully. Little O had come with her grandma, standing out there in the baking hot parking lot. "My tiger wants to wish you good luck on . . ." She started, paused, then started in again. "My tiger wants to wish you good luck on . . . My tiger wants to wish you good luck on . . . your quest!"

The quest then moved on to Cedar Rapids, where we had our first editorial board meeting, with the *Gazette*. Their positive, nicely pitched editorial, which ran a few days later, had a great opening line: "The nuns spoke softly, but they brought a very big bus."[33]

Then it was on to Dubuque, and we were running a little behind schedule and didn't arrive in time for dinner before we hosted our friend-raiser at the Sisters of Charity of the Blessed Virgin Mary. We were so hungry by the time the event was over, I was almost in tears. One restaurant was closed, and another restaurant that would normally have been open was shuttered because they were cleaning rugs. We headed over to the Sisters of the Presentation where we were staying. Casey Schoenberger of Faith in Public Life, who was in charge of all of our press work, pitched in to help wrangle something together with a local NETWORK board member. They found a Subway and brought us sandwiches. I've never tasted anything so good. And the sisters even found wine for us to share—praise God!

As often happens with such happy accidents, that was the beginning of the tradition: after the friend-raiser every night, we would gather with whomever we were staying with and share stories from the bus and drink wine and be community together. That night we spoke of the many sisters who had gathered with other laypeople to join us at the event. The sisters were excited to have their picture taken with the bus. All of us were humbled by the enthusiasm. We learned of the Iowa struggle to create programs for those at the economic margins.

We also made sure that we prayed together every morning. On the second or third day of the tour, when we were exhausted by the pace and novelty of it all, and running to catch up with our schedule, we skipped the joint morning prayer. Big mistake. We thought we were getting extra credit by sleeping in because we would be better out on the road. We were wrong! We were biting and snapping at each other by noon and we knew we couldn't go without praying together again.

The second morning we started at the Dubuque Food Pantry,

same routine, same great response. The food service is a fabulous public-private partnership where the sisters and volunteers could deliver food but in collaboration with the government—it's a very effective, efficient program. That's the kind of thing we need as a nation, and it's the kind of thing the Ryan budget would undermine.

Also in Dubuque we toured Maria House, a collaborative project of six religious organizations that provides transitional housing shelter. We heard from Tia, who at sixteen ran away from a foster placement and was homeless. She thought that the only way she could get housing was by sleeping with men. By the time she was eighteen, she had a one-year-old child and was pregnant with her second child. It was then that she found the homeless shelter run by the sisters in Dubuque. The sisters took her and her child in and supported her during her pregnancy. By the time we met, Tia was nineteen and the mother of two small children. She told us about how the sisters and staff at the shelter had made such a difference in her life. They made sure she got prenatal medical care and helped her learn basic parenting skills. She was almost a child herself, and she hadn't known how to talk to her babies or even play with them, nor did she understand the value of a regular schedule and routine. While at the shelter she got her GED and had enrolled at the community college to get her licensed vocational nurse credential. She planned to go on for her RN degree at a four-year program. She told us that it was only this integrated approach that made a real difference in her life. She was moving into her own place with her children in a supportive housing project sponsored by the sisters. It made all the difference for her and her family. Yet these were the success stories that Congressman Ryan's budget would end. Tia and others like her were the reason we were on the road, and the reason so many responded.

By the time we got to Janesville, Wisconsin—Paul Ryan's hometown, and site of his district office—in midafternoon, there was a huge crowd waiting for us. It was electric, and hot—95 degrees. We sisters were wearing jackets because we quickly found out that people we met wanted to give us stuff—mementos, prayer cards, all sorts of keepsakes. But that meant we needed pockets to put things in, which meant we had to wear jackets. Small price to pay.

The bus parked across the street from Representative Ryan's office, and as we stepped out, we were surrounded by a moving phalanx of TV cameras and a cheering crowd whooping encouragement, singing songs, and waving signs. "What Would Jesus Do? Support the Nuns!" read one. "I stand with the Nuns!" said another. The crowd was so dense that people were spilling out into the street. The police were worried that someone would get hurt and approached Scott Pollard, our bus staff person. Scott was worried that they were going to say we had to send the people home. But no, the police wanted to give us an emergency rally permit and let us use the public square a block away in front of the courthouse. This allowed us to get our message out and keep all our people safe.

We walked into the congressman's office in the Old Towne Mall and met with some of his staffers—it was a lovely meeting, very congenial. They weren't making the mistake Rep. Steve King's staff made. When we came out, I spoke with the press and told them how encouraged I was. "Of course we don't agree on everything, but we were there to lift up a different point of view and say, let's talk," I told the reporters. "If we do invest for the future, we have to take care of things now. We need to be responsible. That's who we are, that's what we think has to happen."

"We each need to exercise responsibility but responsibility only works when we're in solidarity and community," I said. "We're a nation that values individual responsibility but treasures community and we know we can only do it together. That's the same in our faith."

I then thanked the crowd for coming out, they were so ener-
getic and energizing. Then it was off again.[34]

The critics—there were some of those too, usually writing from
their comfortable armchairs—tried to dismiss us because we had
"only" five nuns on the bus, and of course they sniffed that we
were riding in "luxury." They conveniently ignored the fact that
we only had five seats for sisters, and we were rotating in as many
as we could.

But perhaps the most important fact about the nuns and the
bus trip was not what happened on the bus but what happened on
the ground—the legion of nuns who showed up at our events, or
the elderly Immaculate Heart of Mary sisters who lined up outside their motherhouse in Monroe, Michigan, in wheelchairs
and with walkers, holding signs and wearing huge smiles. I have
never been so touched.

This whole trip was a twenty-seven-hundred-mile tribute to
the work of these great religious communities, and of all those
sisters who were laboring away at the works of mercy we sisters
have been doing for decades, centuries. Like the Sister Maura
Brannick Health Center in South Bend, Indiana, where we
stopped on Day Four. It's an inner-city health center that exists
more or less solely because of the energy and devotion of one Holy
Cross nun, Sister Maura Brannick.

Those unseen laborers, and their unseen prayers for us—and
by us for them—were the reason why the Nuns on the Bus became a phenomenon. We were a small outcropping of that great
undersea world of the church that American Catholics, and non-
Catholics, appreciate as the teeming environment where the
church lives out the Word in deeds. The sisters are often unsung,
often underwater, but never unappreciated. Nuns on the Bus was
a hymn to the American sisters even as it sought to further the
mission that the women religious have always pursued—standing

with those who have been left behind, lifting up those who have been oppressed, gathering in those who have been pushed to the margins.

This means people like Billy, whom I met in Milwaukee at St. Benedict the Moor dining room, a Capuchin Franciscan ministry where eighty-five faith-based groups collaborate to provide hot, homemade meals six nights a week for hundreds of people in need. Billy was there with his family when we arrived. He and his wife were working, but the downsized salary still only paid them enough to either feed the family or keep a roof over their heads. They chose the roof so that they could keep their kids in the same school. St. Benedict's was a lifeline, literally. And that was on top of using food stamps for other meals in order to feed their two growing boys.

Later that evening, after meeting Billy and others at the dining hall, we were officially welcomed to Milwaukee by something called the Overpass Light Brigade: it's a network of social activists who came together during the campaign to recall Wisconsin governor Scott Walker in 2011.[35] They make huge letters out of old LED Christmas tree lights attached to a panel and individuals, called "holders of the light," will stand with one letter each on a highway overpass to form a word or phrase.

The Light Brigade welcomed us with a slogan that was just right: "Question Austerity." They even had a bagpiper who piped us up onto the overpass where there were maybe 150 people waiting for us. It was after 9:00 P.M. by the time we got there. Each of us got to hold a letter for a while, to be a "holder of the light." We sang "Happy Birthday" to Sister Mary Wendeln, a Most Precious Blood sister who turned seventy-two that day. She got to hold one of the "E"s and she looked so happy. That evening at the bridge a woman knocked at the door of the bus. Her eighty-five-year-old mother had made us a fruitcake. "She just wanted to support the sisters," she said. I was so tired and touched I almost cried.

When we started the trip, I assumed that the evening friend-raisers would be the time when we would be renewed and stirred up, where we would swap stories and people would laugh at my jokes and life would be fine. And I expected that the places where we would be challenged would be the visits to the places where the sisters worked because that was where the low-income folks were struggling and suffering.

But what I discovered was the opposite: the places where the sisters worked were places that created relationships, beauty, a sense of community; there was a solidarity and mission and connection. Take our press conference in Philadelphia, for example, at the Mercy Neighborhood Ministries. We always trust the people on the ground to recommend whoever they want to speak at the media event, and they told us we should have little Mikhail, a seven-year-old boy from the low-income neighborhood there. I wasn't quite sure he was ready to handle all of the press in the room. He was several inches shorter than the podium, but I handed him the microphone and he walked around in front and said, "I'm Mikhail. I'm a second grader and I am a shining star." He explained that he had been taught that we are all called to be bright lights to guide each other on our journeys. "So, I am a brilliant star." It was fabulous.

But that's the kind of work that gets done in those ministries. Folks are struggling, but people are helping—and they are all in it together. It is the unseen struggle that so many others face, and those were the stories that emerged in the evening at the friend-raisers.

The loneliness, the fear, and the spiritual hunger were huge. Huge. So often I'd come away from friend-raisers and I would just want to weep for all these people trying so hard and still finding themselves so empty.

It was at a friend-raiser in Cincinnati, for example, where I met Jini and Lynn, Margaret Kistler's sister and her partner, who had come from Madison where they lived to a memorial service for Margaret. Margaret lost her life because a few years earlier she lost her job when the recession hit, and when that happened, she lost her health care. And because she didn't have any way to get cancer screening, she ended up dying of colon cancer at the age of fifty-six. Margaret had suspected for two years before her diagnosis that something was wrong. But she couldn't afford to go to the doctor. A trip to the emergency room after a life-threatening episode finally confirmed the diagnosis of cancer—and then it was too late for treatment to help. The disease had spread throughout her body.

So these beautiful women came from Margaret's memorial service, which was held earlier that afternoon, and they brought me her picture. Of course I cry at everything and this was too much. I just wrapped them around me and hugged them and we cried. And they said yes, I could tell Margaret's story because if the health-care reform law is fully implemented—with the full expansion of Medicaid in all the states, which many Republican governors are still resisting—then no more Margarets have to die this way. It's the pro-life thing to do, for God's sake!

The next day when we stopped at House Speaker John Boehner's office in West Chester, on our way to Columbus, we had a good meeting with his staff, and we sold our Faithful budget hard even though we doubted they would adopt it in whole or even in part. It was worth the effort, and important to keep the conversation going. As we were inside we could hear the crowd outside chanting, "Nuns on the Bus!" Two young women who just a day earlier had begun the process of entering the Sisters of Charity came along with us for this leg. When Jean Sammon, one of our NETWORK staffers who was on the bus, asked one of them what she thought, she replied, "Pretty good for my second day in the convent!"

Pretty good for me, too, and I'd been in religious life for decades!

If the bus trip did nothing else, it was a powerful reminder of how much others give us, and teach us, when we think we are doing something for them.

A couple of months later, when I was back to visit Chestnut Hill University, a Catholic college in Philadelphia where we had stopped during the July tour, I met a lovely freshman named Brittany. She and her gaggle of friends came up and asked if they could have my autograph, which I thought was very sweet. It was a big event—more than three hundred people turned out on a sweltering Friday night, battling rush-hour traffic, to be part of the movement. But it's so important amid all the joy of the gathering to focus in on the individuals, and Brittany did that for me that evening.

Then Brittany asked if she could talk to me privately for a minute. After everything was wrapped up, she came over and started telling me how she was the first person in her family to go to college, that she had worked hard to get good grades but that she could only afford the tuition thanks to a federal Pell grant for low-income students. She was terrified that President Obama would not be reelected because under the Republican plans, the Pell grants would be slashed and she would not be able to go back to school.

If that wasn't motivation enough for us to keep pursuing our mission for justice, Brittany then told me that during the summer as she was getting ready for school her mother got arrested—it was something having to do with the mother's boyfriend. But the upshot was that they had no money to bail out the mom, who was stuck in jail in pre-trial detention.

Brittany, an only child, wound up getting evicted. So here is this seventeen-year-old incoming freshman, homeless for a couple of weeks while waiting for the dorm at her new college to open so she would have a place to sleep. And she was recounting all of this very matter-of-factly. Then she told me she got her first paper back from a class in her first semester in college, and she got a B-plus. She burst into tears. It wasn't an A, and she was so afraid that she was letting her mom down, letting down all the teachers who believed in her, that she was not going to be able to succeed in college. What could I do? I just wrapped my arms around this treasure, and said, "Oh my gosh, you are great, you are fine, you are good."

Then I had an idea: I asked for her autograph, so that I could carry her with me. I tore the piece of paper that I had signed for her in half. She signed it, and then she said to me: "Can I put my mom's name too?" She did, and I took it and opened my bible and placed it inside. "I'll carry you with me," I told her. "You'll do fine. You'll do fine."

Brittany will do fine, but only if we help her—and so many like her. And we have to remember that it's not just the children, it's not just the needy. We are all needy. We all need nourishing. Every child needs to see beauty. Every child needs someone to put his or her arms around them. Every child needs someone to hear the story behind the problem. But all of us need that. We all need to stand together. We all need to know that it's safe to tell someone when things are tough. We all need someone to say, "C'mon, you can do it! I will carry *you* in my heart."

It is that hunger—material and emotional and spiritual—that we sisters found in our drive across America over those two weeks and in the connections we made because of the trip. The poor, the working poor, the middle class, and the upper middle class— everyone is starving in some way. It was Ezekiel and the valley of the dry bones. We desperately need nourishment, all of us. We need the prophets to cry out. And we need the people to respond. We can be the miracle that we need, like the Gospel story of the few loaves and fishes that fed the multitude. "Loaves and Fish"

was in fact the poem I wrote after the bus trip, inspired by all that
we saw and prayed over:

> I always joked
> That the miracle of loaves
> And fish was: sharing.
> The women always knew this.
> But in this moment of need
> and notoriety, I ache, tremble
> almost weep at folks so
> hungry, malnourished,
> faced with spiritual famine
> of epic proportions. My heart
> aches with their need.
> Apostlelike, I whine:
> "What are we among so many?
>
> The consistent 2,000-year-old
> ever-new response is:
> "Blessed and broken, you are
> enough." I savor the blessed,
> cower at the broken and
> pray to be enough.

It is this hunger and hope that I marvel at, and in the process
I find joy in the midst of the anguish.

After two weeks, nine states, and twenty-seven hundred miles
on the road, the Nuns on the Bus tour concluded its trip on Monday, July 2, with a final event in Washington, D.C. We had stopped
at thirty-two separate venues, visiting soup kitchens, walk-in
clinics, schools, homeless shelters, and congressional offices.

We even celebrated the Supreme Court's historic decision to uphold the health-care law that we had worked so hard to pass—and that, in many ways, provided the platform for our successful trip. Without our work on health-care reform, the Vatican would not have singled us out for censure; and without that reprimand, we might never have earned the pretrip publicity that gave us such a great liftoff.

Yet as we neared the end of the tour, with so much attention to our mission in the midst of such an intense time for our nation, many people were already asking: "What's next?"

Good question. We knew that NETWORK would never be the same. We couldn't go back to business as usual. What would come next? I had no idea. But I took comfort in my new mantra: "Blessed and broken."

Whatever came next would be the fruit of the Spirit, as it always had been. I had to trust that if we were "blessed and broken," we would be enough for whatever came next. All I knew at that point was that I needed to recharge my spiritual batteries, and soon. I needed a retreat, time to process through prayer. A few weeks later I got that break, but it didn't last long before another call came.

8

~

Speak, and Fear Not

My path from the bus tour to a prime-time speaking slot at the 2012 Democratic National Convention was not a straight road by any stretch of the imagination. It had plenty of potholes. That seems to be the way that life, and the Holy Spirit, work. It is certainly the way political campaigns function, especially in a tight presidential race, where every day, every hour, can change the dynamic of the contest and force strategists to recalibrate their needs.

What the Obama campaign apparently needed in August, in the weeks before the convention, was to underscore the issues we had raised during the bus trip—issues of justice and family values that had connected so viscerally with so many people, in part because we presented them from a perspective of faith, not ideology.

So with the buzz about the bus still humming in the political ether, I received an e-mail from the campaign's faith outreach people asking for the names of Catholic sisters who might be willing to pray at the convention. That made sense: the social justice focus of the nuns often coincided with the policies—or at least the ideals—of the Democratic Party. This alignment was especially clear in the Great Depression and through the New Deal era that reshaped America's view of society's role toward caring for the less fortunate. The Catholic Church's leaders, and rank-and-file Catholics, once saw those reforms as putting core elements of Catholic social teaching into practice, and they cast their votes accordingly. Not anymore. Catholics are still the largest voting bloc among all faith groups, accounting for nearly a quarter of the votes cast in presidential elections. But since the days of Ronald Reagan, Catholics have become a genuine swing vote. Whoever won Catholics won the White House. Catholics were the key, and once again they were in play—for both sides.

I gave the Obama campaign some names, and they then came back and asked me if I would be willing to give the prayer myself. "I pray a lot and I could probably handle that," I told them.

There was an immediate precedent for taking on such a role: at the historic 2008 convention in Denver that first nominated Barack Obama, St. Joseph Sister Catherine Pinkerton, who was eighty-six and a longtime lobbyist for NETWORK, delivered a prayer that closed the convention. "I didn't know if I wanted to do that or not," Catherine said at the time. "I thought, 'What have I got to lose?' It's my right to do that as an American citizen." Besides, bishops and priests regularly delivered invocations and benedictions at the conventions of both parties.[36]

Catherine also said she was inspired by the excitement the campaign generated among young people. "A lot of the young people with whom I'm working went double-barreled into it (the campaign)," she told Catholic News Service. "I thought if the young people are seeing something here and these are young kids immersed in Catholic theology and social teaching, then there's something to this."

Four years later there was still something to be said for that rationale, maybe even more so. With the economic suffering persisting, and Republicans in Congress blocking every effort at progress—while offering their fatally flawed Ryan budget as the only piece of legislation they were willing to pass—the nation needed to hear a different perspective, and one rooted in faith.

I said sure, I'll do it. Catherine had received some blowback for taking on the task, and no doubt I would too. But it was nothing we couldn't handle, and the opportunity was clearly worth it. Besides, we at NETWORK had tried to interest the Republicans in allowing us to offer a social justice workshop for delegates at their convention, which was to be held August 27–30 in Tampa. We were planning to lead two such events at the Democratic Convention. But the GOP never responded to our many requests, nor did they make any invitation for me to pray at the convention.

In late August, a few days after the DNC's initial invitation to offer a prayer at the convention, I was in France trying to squeeze in a preconvention respite near the wonderful ecumenical monastic community of Taizé when one of our staff from the NETWORK office called. She said the Obama campaign was trying to get hold of me again to see if I would give not a prayer but an address at the convention! This was a remarkable opportunity to set out our vision of justice to a national, even global, audience. Was it okay if they contacted me? Well, sure, I said.

Thanks to the complications of differing time zones, and stretches of radio silence for personal prayer and meditation, communication was a bit difficult. But I finally reached my contacts at the campaign and said that yes I would be happy to speak if I could do three things: talk about the people at the economic margins of our society, say that I'm pro-life, and tell the audience that we stand for the 100 percent and that the Democrats need to have a big tent too.

They said they'd pass that along and the response came back right away—yes, yes, that was all fine. On the trip home on the airplane I wrote the first draft of the speech. I typed it up when I got back to Washington and sent it to the speech committee. The committee sent back a revision that basically turned it into a political speech, which was totally unacceptable to me. This was less than a week before the convention, which was to start on September 3 and would end on September 6.

I e-mailed them back and said, in effect, "Look, if you want a political speech, get a political person. I think my value added for you is that I come at it from a perspective of faith. That's how I do it. And quite frankly, I'm happy to give up my space at the Democratic National Convention because the whole thing is getting challenging for me on a personal level."

What I meant by that "challenging," and what no one knew, was that word of my plans to pray, or give a speech, at the Democratic Convention had reached the leadership of my community before I had a chance to speak with them, and they were not happy.

Much of the problem stemmed from issues of communications and logistics, and it was further complicated by the unpredictability of campaign politics, and Church politics.

On August 22, a Wednesday, Mitt Romney let slip—during an interview with the conservative Catholic cable channel, EWTN, no surprise—that he had invited Cardinal Timothy Dolan of New York to deliver the closing blessing at the Republican Convention, and Dolan had accepted. This was seen as a coup for Romney; not that anyone doubted the political leanings of the bishops, but by custom it was usually the bishop of the diocese where a convention was held who received an invitation from the party holding its convention in his backyard. As president of the United States Conference of Catholic Bishops, Cardinal Dolan was the leader of the American hierarchy and having him on board was a big deal for the Republicans.[37]

Dolan's presence also put pressure on the DNC to counter that move. There was already a growing campaign on social media to have me appear at the convention, hence one reason for the initial invitation for me to give a prayer. But the convention planners for the Democrats were also working behind the scenes to see if they could secure Dolan to give the final benediction to close the convention. There were some concerns about whether the Democratic delegates would behave, and whether they would accord the cardinal the sort of reception that would make his appearance a positive capstone to the renomination of Barack Obama. But those worries didn't stop the campaign from moving ahead with the invitation.

So on August 28, a Tuesday, just as the Republicans were kicking off their convention in Florida, Cardinal Dolan announced that he had accepted an invitation to deliver the closing prayer for the Democrats the following week in Charlotte, just as he was doing that week for the Republicans in Tampa.

As I was flying back from retreat in Taize, the Obama campaign announced (three days earlier than planned) that I was going to address the convention on Wednesday, the night before President Obama was to be officially nominated and Dolan would give his closing blessing.[38]

The upshot was that I had not processed it with my community, and they found out about my appearance just like everyone else did, through a press release and news reports. The leadership was upset, feeling left out, and fearful about whether this could hurt the wider community of the Sisters of Social Service. So the leadership council wrote a letter to our vowed members and associates asking me not to speak at the Democratic Convention.

It was all very hurtful and disconcerting, to say the least. But it was a gift too. I immediately began receiving powerful messages of support from other members of the community urging me to go ahead with the DNC talk. One of my sisters wrote in the first of many group e-mail responses to the leadership council's recommendation:

I believe that backing away from an opportunity to advance the work of Simone, Network, and all who have committed themselves to the poor and marginalized out of fear would not be true to the Gospel or to our Charism. Sometimes we must do the difficult thing. My prayers are with Simone, Network, and all of you.

The responses all recognized the concerns raised by the leadership, and their good faith in wanting to protect the community above all, and me in particular, and to keep us apart from the partisan fray that was dividing both our Church and our society. But they also pointed out that NETWORK had tried to find a place at the Republican Convention, that we—like Cardinal Dolan—were not endorsing Democrats (or anyone else), and that this sort of involvement was part of our mission as Sisters of Social Service. It had been from our founding by Sister Margaret Slachta and must remain so today. As one of my sisters wrote:[39]

As descendants of Margaret, we are called to this kind of courage. It is the center of our religious DNA. In a world where institutions at every level are failing people in their tenuous hold on survival, I believe that the world looks to us for this courage that questions, challenges and confronts while insisting all the while that there is room at the table for everyone. Nowhere is this witness more needed than

in the political arena, whose contours are shaped by the
self-interest of the very rich and carried on the backs of the
poorest . . . I'm grateful that Simone is in a position where
she can reframe the distorted religious lens that is being
applied by some to our nation's priorities. I ask that we continue the trust that we placed in her when she accepted this
position, and act from the Pentecost call that is now pro-
phetically in our midst.

Wrote another:

My dearest Simone: Yes! I echo the many positive responses
that so many have made for this decision. It can't have been
an easy one to make, but so very necessary at this time in
our lives. Sometimes it is the most unexpected voice that
will make the most unexpected impact on the least expected heart. You can make the difference and be the voice
that someone needs to hear.

Even one of our more conservative members spoke out mov-
ingly on behalf of our decision:

I am so proud to be part of a community and tradition that
can bring forth women like Sr. Simone. She didn't spring
up overnight out of an abyss. Besides offering our prayers
for the care and safety of this community, I would ask us to
consider how we can actively support our sister and this tradition of courage in the trials that will most probably follow.
    I believe that this is an opportunity to speak up for those
whose voices have been silenced—the marginalized, those
impoverished, women, the working poor, children, immigrants and even women religious.

Said another: "I do not underestimate the seriousness of this issue, nor do I think this is an easy choice." But she said that the opportunity for a woman's voice to be heard on such an occasion, and one that comes from the heart of the Church, where women are so often not heard, was vitally important.

Even one of the sisters who at first weighed in against my DNC appearance soon changed her mind, citing her "life-changing experience" with the Nuns on the Bus tour: "SPEAK and fear not," she wrote.

The community was overwhelmingly in support of my speaking at the convention, and without the controversy, I'd never have known the depth and breadth of that feeling. It was truly a gift.

Still, I needed to process the whole episode for myself and make sure that what I was doing was the right thing for the community, for women religious in the United States, and for the people whose difficulties we wanted to raise up during the bus trip.

The first two days of September also happened to be Labor Day weekend. Every Labor Day weekend for thirty years I have gathered with a group of sisters, brothers, and priests who are lawyers. It is a time of spiritual reflection and contemplation, not much in the way of legal strategizing. This year's retreat could not have come at a better time—after some of the most intense days of my entire life as a religious, and just ahead of what was likely to be one of the most intense moments of my life in the public square.

That Friday afternoon, August 31, the woman who was leading the group invited us to an experience of what she called "contemplative intercessory prayer." I'd never heard of that. I do contemplative prayer but generally not intercessory prayer. In most intercessory prayer you tell God what to fix and how to do it. I actually find that notion mildly amusing. In contemplative intercessory prayer, however, you put someone you are worried about in the center of your concern, and rather than telling God what ought to happen, you open yourself and say, "Holy Spirit, what are you asking me to do, or be, or say for them?" Then you sit with that for a while and after a while let other people migrate into your awareness.

My prayer was to ask God whether I should heed the request of the leadership council of our community and pass on the speaking opportunity at the Democratic Convention. I said, and I meant, that I was willing to do that if called to do so. I waited in silence. The time passed, and nothing. Silence. Then people we had met on the bus began to wander into my consciousness: Margaret and Billy, little Mikhail and Matt and Mark, all the sisters, all the wonderful people who supported us at the stops along the way and in silent prayer and support across the country.

I then asked the question, "What would you like me to do on their behalf?" In two seconds came the thundering response: "SPEAK! SPEAK!" It was so powerful I just started to cry, sitting there in that contemplative circle.

From that moment on it was 100 percent clear to me that I had to speak up for them. On Sunday, September 2, I wrote to the community and explained my decision. I noted that the staff of the Leadership Conference of Women Religious, who were under investigation by the Vatican, said they were supportive of my planned appearance and did not think it would affect their discussions with Rome.

I felt at peace, knowing that the members of my community supported me, and above all that I was being faithful to the people we met on the bus trip and to the Spirit's challenge to me. I had to stand up there and speak for those who had no voice in that convention, and in our political system.

What I also wrote to the community in my September 2 e-mail was that after I told the DNC that their changes to my speech draft were unacceptable, they responded right away saying, "No, no, we didn't mean to do that. It's your speech. Write what you want in order to make it yours." It was going to be a speech about faith, and the community need not worry about me becoming a political operative.

So I adjusted the speech utilizing some of the speech committee's suggestions, but I kept it focused on faith and justice. I sent it back in and headed to Charlotte. The convention handlers did a great job prepping us. I got in two half-hour sessions, on Tuesday and then on Wednesday morning, hours before I was to deliver the speech. The prep team rehearsed us in a room down in bowels of the Charlotte arena. We had a speech coach, two speechwriters, and a teleprompter operator. I'd never used a teleprompter before, except the Friday before when I taped a public service announcement. What a gift to have had at least that one brief thirty-second experience!

We went over the speech, tightened it up some more, and then at the second practice session tightened it still further. I agreed with the changes even though it meant leaving out a couple of the stories from the bus trip. But I felt good about the speech, and there was so much else going on to distract me from my anxiety over what I was going to say and how I was going to do it. I mean, more than twenty-five million people were watching live that night, boosting the convention's ratings above even the game between the Dallas Cowboys and the New York Giants that opened the NFL season! We were bigger than football, at least for one night.[40]

There were also plenty of celebrity pols around to keep my mind from focusing too much on my own task. I did one of my practice sessions right after Elizabeth Warren, which was very cool. Then on that Wednesday night, when we were in the "green room" waiting our turn to go onstage, all these volunteers and various notables were coming in asking to have their picture taken with me. It was so surprising, and moving. But it also messed with my makeup! And television is intense. Makeup has to be dramatic in order to neutralize the bright camera lights, but it succumbed to the embraces of so many supporters. Luckily one of the last stops before you go out is called "makeup repair," and those folks had a lot to do.

Then, as I waited in the wings by the curtain, the very last moment before you are propelled alone onto the stage, there was a tall, thoughtful man tasked with giving final instructions. He was wonderful. He took a minute to walk me behind the press gallery to look out at the arena and told me, "Just own the house. Just own the house. It's yours." Funny advice for a sister who has taken a vow of poverty, but I got what he meant. He pointed up to a big screen that was showing the governor of Colorado, John Hickenlooper, who was speaking before me. "See what a big smile can do?" he said. "Just smile, enjoy it." He asked me some questions to see how my voice was doing, to check if my mouth was dry or I needed water.

As the moment approached he told me to take some deep breaths. "I can do that, I do Zen," I told him. "Perfect," he said, "just center."

He put his hand on my shoulder and said that when it was time to go on he would give me a little push. But I was not to look back at him, he said. I was to just go out and take it all in. So I did. I walked out there, and as much as I had prepared, I was stunned. People knew who I was when they announced my name, an arena filled with more than twenty thousand people, all cheering wildly. That I got such a response was shocking. *Oh my glory*, I thought. *This is amazing.*

Then it grew quiet.

During the prep sessions, the coaches had told me that there were thousands of people in the arena and most of them would be talking among themselves, even during the main speeches. I'd seen that was the case and knew a speaker couldn't take it personally. The delegates had so much to talk about, so many different things to do, that only some portion of them, at most, would pay attention to the podium. The handlers told me not to be surprised, but to think of the hum in the arena as a river. You just have to speak over the river—that's the background noise. Speak to the television audience, they said.

Well, suddenly I was out there onstage and there was no hum. It was like, whoa, WHAT HAPPENED TO THE RIVER?

Come, Holy Spirit! I said to myself, and I launched in:

Good evening, I'm Sister Simone Campbell, and I'm one of the "nuns on the bus." So, yes, we have nuns on the bus. And a nun on the podium!

Let me explain why I'm here tonight. In June, I joined other Catholic sisters on a 2,700-mile bus journey through nine states to tell Americans about the budget that Congressman Paul Ryan wrote and Governor Romney endorsed.

Paul Ryan claims this budget reflects the principles of our shared faith. But the United States Conference of Catholic Bishops stated that the Ryan budget failed a basic moral test, because it would harm families living in poverty.

We agree with our bishops, and that's why we went on the road: to stand with struggling families and to lift up our Catholic sisters who serve them. Their work to alleviate suffering would be seriously harmed by the Romney-Ryan budget, and that is wrong.

During our journey, I rediscovered a few truths. First, Mitt Romney and Paul Ryan are correct when they say that each individual should be responsible. But their budget goes astray in not acknowledging that we are responsible not only for ourselves and our immediate families. Rather, our faith strongly affirms that we are all responsible for one another. I am my sister's keeper! I am my brother's keeper!

While we were in Toledo, I met ten-year-old twins Matt and Mark, who had gotten into trouble at school for fighting. Sister Virginia and the staff at the Padua Center took them in when they were suspended and discovered on a home visit that these ten-year-olds were trying to care for their bedridden mother who has MS and diabetes.

They were her only caregivers. The sisters got her medical help and are giving the boys some stability. Now the boys are free to claim much of the childhood that they were losing. Clearly, we all share responsibility for the Matts and Marks in our nation.

In Milwaukee, I met Billy and his wife and two boys at St. Benedict's dining room. Billy's work hours were cut back in the recession and Billy is taking responsibility for himself and his family. But right now without food stamps, he and his wife could not put food on their family table.

We share responsibility for creating an economy where parents with jobs earn enough to care for their families. In order to cut taxes for the wealthy, the Romney-Ryan budget would make it even tougher for hardworking Americans like Billy to feed their families. Paul Ryan says this budget is in keeping with the moral values of our shared faith. I disagree.

In Cincinnati, I met Jini, who had just come from her sister's memorial service. When Jini's sister Margaret lost her job, she lost her health insurance. She developed cancer and had no access to diagnosis or treatment. She died unnecessarily, and that is tragic. And it is wrong.

The Affordable Care Act will cover people like Margaret. We all share responsibility to ensure that this vital health-care reform law is properly implemented and that all governors—all governors—expand Medicaid coverage so no more Margarets die from lack of care. This is part of my pro-life stance and the right thing to do.

I have so many other stories to tell. But I'll only tell you one more. In Hershey, Pennsylvania, a woman in her late thirties came to me, approached us. She asked for the names of some people she could talk to, because she felt alone and isolated. Her neighbors have been polarized by politics masquerading as values. She cares about the well-being of her people in her community.

She wishes the rest of the nation would listen to one another with kindness and compassion. Listen to one another rather than yell at each other. I told her then, and I tell her now, that she is not alone.

Looking out at you tonight, I feel your presence combined with that of the thousands of caring people we met on our journey. Together, we understand that an immoral budget that hurts already struggling families does not reflect our nation's values. We are better than that.

So I urge you, I urge you—join us on the bus. Join us as together we stand with Matt and Mark, Billy and his family, the woman in Hershey, and the Margarets of our nation.

This is what nuns on the bus are all about: we care for the 100 percent, and that will secure the blessings of liberty to ourselves and our nation. So join us, join us, as we nuns on the bus, all of us, drive for faith, family, and fairness. Thank you so much!

Less than seven minutes onstage, fewer than eight hundred words on the page, and an absolutely overwhelming experience.[41]

At first I was surprised at the silence in the arena. But then, as I dove in, there was this reflexive response from the crowd. They were listening, and then clapping, and then cheering at all the most powerful moments. It just felt connected. And, most important, we were able to lift up our people in that remarkable setting, people who would otherwise not be able to be there. That's part of the reason I wasn't nervous. Those voices needed to be there. I was speaking for them. The Spirit did the rest and made it this amazing thing, for all of us.

In fact I heard later that because I mentioned Matt and Mark, the twins from Toledo, the local television station in Ohio went to their middle school and did a story on them. Their friends started calling them "Mr. Hollywood." They were really excited.

The impact of the speech was immediate, and obvious, and amusing to a Catholic sister who'd never imagined herself in such a venue. Back in the green room, Governor Jack Markell of Delaware, who spoke after me, came over and introduced himself. "I hear you're a tough act to follow," he said. "No, no, no," I reassured him. "I'm sure you'll be just fine." Then I saw him after the speeches were done, as we speakers were all together signing posters and such for Democratic National Committee members and the presidential library and what not. "How'd it go for you?" I asked him. He looked down and shook his head with a smile: "Not as well as it went for you." That was very sweet.

The next night, of course, President Obama accepted the nomination with a wonderful speech. We up in the "nose-bleed section" of the arena were ecstatic when he said that poverty was an issue in our country! It was one of the few times that he had said the word and referred to the disturbing truth in our nation. We believe that our bus trip helped make that happen. To us it indicated that we were having an impact by shaping the conversation.

Right after the president, Cardinal Dolan delivered the closing blessing. Fears of a chilly reception were entirely unfounded. The arena was attentive and truly prayerful as the cardinal spoke, touching on so many of the same themes that I spoke about the night before. I was holding my breath about what he would say and how it would be received, but it wound up as another moving moment of Catholic witness at this convention.

The Saturday following the convention I was catching up on work at my desk in DC when my cell phone rang. A man's voice asked if this was "Sister Simone Campbell." I said that it was and he asked: "Can you hold for the president of the United States." Of course I said yes. The president called to thank me not only for the speech at the DNC, but also, he said, for our lifting up the reality of struggling families. In that conversation, I got to thank him for saying the word poverty in his acceptance speech, and I urged him to make more of it. He ended by saying that he hoped that we would have a chance to talk policy in the not-too-distant future. It was amazing to have the opportunity to influence our national engagement with one of the most critical issues of our time. I was grateful yet again to be making a difference in this challenging time.

The next two months, the home-stretch run of an overlong, hugely expensive presidential race was intense, to say the least.

But we also know—or ought to know—that for all the drama and hard work of a campaign, an election is the easy part. It's only a choice of yes or no, one or two, A or B. Keeping people engaged in developing and implementing policy is the tough part. Policy is hard; keeping people engaged in policy is really hard.

On Sunday, January 20, 2013, the day before President Obama was inaugurated and sworn in for a second term, I spoke at a meeting of Organizing for America. The Democrats had set up OFA (Organizing for America) after Obama's first inauguration as a way to promote the administration's legislative priorities with grassroots activism.

At this event there were four thousand people, mainly young campaign staffers and volunteers who they were trying to convert from election people to policy people. I was frank with them: policy is much harder because policy is more complex than campaigning, and not as exciting. You are never, ever going to have the up or down victory. You, and your opponents, will always be able to fight another day. And if you are successful, it will be because you found the best way forward, and that path will always be across some middle ground.

There is no magic deadline with policy, no arbitrary date after which you go home or go party. If you do pass a law, you then have to protect it. Health-care reform is a good example. Yes, it was a great victory. But it immediately came under assault, in the courts and in Congress. If the court battle was largely successful, the legislative and regulatory efforts to undermine the law continue, in Washington and in the states.

Obama's victory in November of 2012 was inspiring to his supporters, and good for them. But the events of 2013—and the political positioning and posturing as we headed toward the crucial midterm elections in the fall of 2014—showed how critical it was to master policy and governance if justice for the American people was not to be delayed, or denied.

9

Nuns on the Border

There are two things that shut down the contemplative life: fear and grasping.

Fear is a pretty obvious threat, or at least it is one that I have recognized most often in myself. When I am afraid, I curl in on myself and do not pay attention to others. I try to protect myself like a snail pulled into its shell. But grasping has been a little more difficult for me to come to understand. At first, I saw grasping as the reaction to fear when my instinct is to be protective and stay with what I know. But I have discovered that grasping can also occur with the good things in life that happen. Having favorite memories, holding on to treasures, wanting to live in the past are all ways of grasping what has been rather than living life now. I find it hard to imagine sometimes that new good experiences will come my way. I am tempted to just savor the past experiences. But what I have learned is that if I am holding on too tightly to even the good things of my life, I have no room for the new. I have to stay openhanded—welcoming new opportunities, new needs, new fears, new joys.

So, after the first bus trip, and the out-of-nowhere success in broadcasting our message, I never thought that there would be another. How could there be? We were so convinced this was a one-off gift of the Spirit that we didn't even do a standard post-event evaluation with the Markham Group that had provided the bus and staff. But after the 2012 election and President Obama's reelection, we also knew that immigration reform would likely be a priority for Congress. If that was the case, we knew that we would need to use every possible resource to make this sorely needed reform happen. Millions of immigrants were living in fear, in the shadows, and at the margins—which is where we sisters find the ground of our being. Nuns on the bus also had to be nuns on the border, if that's what was needed.

Republicans, on the other hand, had not been thinking that way. The GOP had historically resisted immigration reform because they knew that most new immigrants begin by voting for Democrats. After the 2012 November election, however, many of the top-ranking Republicans also knew that if they did not develop a more open approach to immigrants and people of color, they were not going to have a politically viable party in the coming decades. The Democrats were on board, of course, and soon Senate Republicans and some of their colleagues in the House, aided by the Republican National Committee, also began to work on comprehensive immigration reform.

The debate was driven by several major realities about immigration in this country:

- An estimated eleven million people have been living in the United States without current immigration papers. As many as six million of these people have overstayed some temporary visa (visitor, student, worker, etc.). More than half of this number have been in the United States for more than ten years.[42] So the immigrant population is well integrated into communities all over the country.

- A quota system limits the number of immigrants per year to 226,000 for family-related visas and 150,000 for business-related visas.[43] These numbers are far below either what families or the economy need. In fact, it is so bad that if you are the brother or sister of a Filipino American, the wait for your petition to come up is about eighteen years![44] Then you can wait another two to three years just for your interview.

- Then there is the issue of temporary workers, especially for the agriculture industry. Since September 11, 2001, security screening policies have made it very difficult to process papers for temporary workers. Consequently, farmers have not been able to harvest their crops and have experienced tremendous losses. These processes need to be streamlined.

- The toughest policy issue is regulating the "future flow" of immigrants into our country. We need some process that is flexible and predictable while accommodating the needs of families and business.

- Finally, the issue of border security is a perennial issue. In the unsuccessful attempt at comprehensive reform in 2007, the argument was made that there should be an "enforcement first" strategy.[45] Although this was not adopted as the specific policy, it was in fact what happened. The United States has spent $3.5 billion on security between the Mexican and U.S. border in 2012 alone.[46] The questions now are: Should more be done? Are there other security measures that should be put in place?

In the spring of 2013, a "Gang of Eight" in the Senate submitted a bipartisan bill that addressed the principal issues. We in the interfaith community went into high gear to support and improve the measure and we were joined—with greater urgency than ever before—by conservative Evangelicals as well as by groups like the U.S. Chamber of Commerce, the Small Business Association, and organized labor. We were all in favor of comprehensive immigration reform with a path to citizenship for the undocumented. But politics is not always responsive to such unanimity, and at NETWORK we knew that it was going to be a hard struggle going forward, and we knew that we had to put every resource into the fight.

So we decided to rev up the bus and go back on the road. We wanted to do for immigration in 2013 what we had done for poverty and income inequality in 2012—put it front and center in the national debate in hopes that laws and policies would follow from that.

Our message this time: "Comprehensive Immigration reform NOW!!" This time we planned to make the trip much longer—a total of sixty-eight hundred miles over three weeks, with stops in fifteen states—an itinerary that mirrored how broad and diverse our country is, geographically and culturally and ethnically, and highlighted how silly it was to ignore that immigration had transformed our nation in every generation, and for the better. Immigration is the story of America, and to deny immigration is to deny ourselves.

We decided that since Republicans were key to this policy change, we wanted to support those Republicans who were in the Gang of Eight (Senators Graham, Rubio, McCain, and Flake) while also encouraging others (including House members) on the issue. We also wanted to bolster Democratic senators who faced blowback in their districts. That's why we chose a route that did not run through the part of the country where we had the majority of our supporters but one that went down the East Coast and through a lot of southern states, including North and South Carolina, Georgia, Florida, Alabama, Louisiana, and Texas. That said, I liked to call Texas "the new Ohio" because immigration is transforming the Lone Star State to such a degree that it could be a swing state as early as 2016. We traveled the frontier of that metamorphosis: along the border in Laredo and El Paso, through Nogales in Arizona and San Ysidro in California. Finally, we headed up the California coast through Orange County—past the region where my own parents had moved decades ago, and where I was raised, a first-generation Californian—and then up the San Joaquin valley and key Republican districts.

All along the sixty-eight hundred miles and three weeks we visited sisters and other faith-based groups that worked with and for immigrant communities, lobbied senators and representatives, held press conferences, and gave interviews; and in the evenings, we did our friend-raisers just as we did on the first trip. Although there were many similarities with the first time around, there was much that was different.

It took me a few days to realize one key difference. In 2012, the bus trip aimed to push back against bad things happening to good people and good programs. Everywhere we went on that first trip we saw good programs that would be decimated by the Republican budget put forward by Paul Ryan and his supporters. The bus became a beacon of hope and protection for these programs. As we drove from town to town in 2013, though, I realized that we were on the road to lift up a broken system. At almost every stop we met fine people who had extremely painful stories. Every day we walked into anguish and tried to hold our hearts open to the suffering. Some days were harder than others, and a few times I just broke down and cried.

A second difference: even though we were going through the South and traditionally Republican territory, we encountered little of the hostility to our bus and our cause that I had expected.

Our bus drivers did encounter some negativity at the various truck stops where we fueled up and got food. But we did not experience much in the way of open protests. In Florida, a small group did come to one of our evening events as "dissenters." But they were concerned about Church issues and not immigration and were not disruptive. The same happened in Austin. Finally, in Phoenix, a few people showed up who were actually protesting our position on immigration.

And a final, startling difference: during this trip, we had five bishops who came to five different events, and in some places we were able to hold our events in parishes with the support of the local diocese. This was a sea change.

I will never forget the night in Lawrenceville, New Jersey, when Bishop David O'Connell came to our friend-raiser, sat in the front row, and asked to have his picture taken with me! He was ill and in a lot of pain—vulnerable but strong, I wrote to a friend. And from that strength he spoke from the heart about our shared mission on behalf of the immigrant in our land.

Such a far cry from the experience on the first bus trip! It struck me that a big reason for this change is the fact that in Francis we have a new pope who also cares about these issues and speaks up for them. Our bishops do not need to be looking over their shoulders so much when the Bishop of Rome has their backs.

For me, the enduring image of this trip was to go from Ellis Island in the New York Harbor to Angel Island in San Francisco Bay. Many people don't know that Angel Island, "the Ellis Island of the West," is where Chinese and other Asian immigrants were held while awaiting processing.

At our closing press conference there, on June 18, 2013, after three weeks and thousands of miles, Craig Wong of Grace Fellowship Community Church told the story of his grandmother, Wong Shee, who arrived there nearly a century earlier. She had fled her country in the throes of civil war and famine, forced to leave her only son, and seeking to reunite with her husband who had left ahead of her to start a shop in San Francisco's Chinatown.

On October 31, 1916, her ship reached Angel Island. But instead of a gateway she entered a trap: frightened and disoriented, she was shoved into a 30-by-30-foot room with a hundred other women. "The food was bad, the conditions unsanitary," her grandson told us that day. "Worst of all was being separated from her husband, not knowing if she'd ever see him again. What stood between her and her husband was the interrogation, an insufferable quest to prove her identity as a merchant's wife. This wore on for months to the brink of suicide, as many others had done."

It was this "two-faced America," as Craig called it, that inspired the bitter laments etched on the walls of the detention cells. They are still visible today, reflections like this one:

America has power, but not justice. In prison, we are victimized as if we are guilty. Given no opportunity to explain, it is brutal. I bow my head in reflection but there is nothing I can do. Imprisoned in the wooden building day after day, my freedom withheld, how can I bear to talk about it? I am anxious and depressed and cannot fall asleep. The days are long and bottle constantly empty; my sad mood is not dispelled. Nights are long and the pillow cold; who can pity my loneliness?

Two Presbyterian sisters, Ethel Higgins and Donaldina Cameron, eventually lobbied for his grandmother's release, and their Christian witness all those years ago is one we need to replicate today.

The "national schizophrenia," as Craig Wong put it, that reduces people to commodities who we bring in when it helps us economically and then bar when we fear it hurts us—whatever the reality of the formula—is part and parcel of our history.

That is why we also went to Charleston, South Carolina, and the slave market museum. We wanted to acknowledge the dark heart of our history—honoring the fact that not everyone came to this country voluntarily, and only on the terms of the powerful. The sin of slavery still echoes in our society and we wanted to commit ourselves to never allowing a policy that creates a permanent underclass. For us, this means that all undocumented people in our country need an earned path to citizenship.

On this trip we also wanted to see the border and understand the diverse dynamics that exist in the different crossing points. Finally we wanted to understand the impact on the Native American tribes who live along our southern border. It was a big trip with many goals, but the most important aim was to advocate for comprehensive immigration reform now.

We started that first night with a "bus blessing" in the cold rain in New Haven, Connecticut, and then headed off to New Jersey to stay the night with the Dominican sisters near the Statue of Liberty. We were one of the first groups to get a permit for Liberty Park after the 2012 Superstorm Sandy had devastated the region. Of course I had worried about many things in preparing for the trip—chief among them was the worry that at the end of the tour we would not be able to see Angel Island in San Francisco Bay because of the notorious fog that so often blankets the water in June. I had not, however, had even a moment's worry about fog in New York harbor! But when we arrived at Liberty Park, Ellis Island was in fact shrouded in a late spring haze and the Statue of Liberty was not even visible. Undaunted, we went ahead with our kickoff news conference.

It was our first public event, and we made it an interfaith event to reflect the spectrum of groups behind immigration reform and also present in the immigrant community. And lo and behold, in the middle of our rally the sun came out! It dazzled us for the next sixty-eight hundred miles as well, and became the symbol of blessing. On the other hand, be careful what you pray for: farther down the road in Texas and Arizona I did pine a bit for a cool, fog-shrouded day as a respite from the intense heat in the Southwest. But that first day in New Jersey, we knew we were off to a good start.

Later, in Scranton, Pennsylvania, we were welcomed by the mayor, the Sisters of the Immaculate Heart of Mary and a multitude of immigrants and longtime residents of the area. The mayor told us that Scranton had actually benefited from anti-immigrant laws in the neighboring town of Hazelton. He reported that the immigrants had moved into Scranton and created an economic boom as new businesses opened and new opportunities emerged for all of the residents of this Rust Belt community. It turns out that there are over thirty languages that are the first language of at least one student in the Scranton high school. The immigrant community had brought fabulous food to share, and I got to taste my first Bhutanese dumpling. It would be worth it to return to Scranton just to get a second dumpling!

The side of the bus this time around was plastered with our slogan: "Raise your hands! Raise your voice! For Comprehensive Immigration Reform NOW!" And that very first full day we sisters started putting the slogan into practice at each stop, getting everyone at our rallies to actually raise their hands and voices. The result is that there are a million pictures of us with our hands raised and our mouths open in the process of nurturing an advocacy community. It became the chant that followed us all across the country.

We also developed a rhythm of sisters on the bus speaking at various events. We tried to make sure that everyone got to speak at least once a day at one of our public events. We had room this time for ten sisters on the bus. I think we were a "full house" all along the way. Three of us (Sister Elaine Betencourt, CSJ, Sister

Mary Ellen Lacy, DC, and I) rode the whole trip. We had about forty others who rotated through for part of the trip. My big joy was that four sisters from my own community were able to ride along for a significant part of the trip.

The second full day on the road, we went to Camden, New Jersey, which has struggled against poverty and urban decay for decades. But that tagline of failure can obscure the human stories of success.

For example, we got to meet some seventh graders who are doing an amazing job of community organizing to improve their neighborhood. They showed us how they had cleaned up their neighborhood park, and while we were there they saw a swing that was broken and picked up a cell phone and called the park director, whom they know very well. They told us that they meet every month with park officials, the mayor, and the police to make sure things are being done for the neighborhood. They then showed us the mural that they had painted. They explained how they got paint from the city parks department and then made the mural with their art teacher and covered it with a slick surface so that nobody could put graffiti on it. When people from the suburbs come to see them, they often ask, "Can we give you money?" The kids say, "No thanks." What they really want, they said, is for the people from the suburbs to call City Hall and find out why city officials aren't doing their job. The kids say that they shouldn't have to raise money to do the city's job. We saw their success and heard them talk about how they had organized to get the city to allocate $60,000 to light the park. But they quickly told us it wasn't just for their park because they wanted to improve the other Camden parks for other kids to enjoy. This group of mostly immigrant kids was doing fabulous work to improve their neighborhood and exercise democracy.

At our events we tried to include a Spanish-language element when possible, and I quickly learned how important that was to getting our message out. At an event on the second day, in Washington, where we were joined by labor representatives backing immigration reform, Frank Sherry of America's Voice came to the microphone and asked me to say a few words in Spanish. It was a surprise to me, but with a prayer to the Holy Spirit (and no time to be nervous) I walked up and spoke in Spanish for the Spanish-language press. I must have done okay—afterward, at least a half-dozen Spanish-speaking reporters wanted to interview me about our trip and our goals, which brought Nuns on the Bus to a whole new audience.

After that rally, at the Methodist building across the street from the U.S. Capitol, I was invited to the White House to meet with President Obama. When I had seen him at the Easter Prayer Breakfast at the White House a few weeks before, I told him that we were going on the road again. I knew that immigration reform was a priority for him and he told me he was going to follow us "every step of the way." So when we came to Washington, he wanted to meet with me to show his support for our work.

I've been to the White House a number of times but had never been to the Oval Office. It's always an impressive thing to meet the president of the United States, but while waiting in the reception area in the West Wing, I saw some people whom I had come to know during my years in the capital, and that helped put me at ease. Agriculture Secretary Tom Vilsack came over and greeted me, and Health and Human Services Secretary Kathleen Sebelius was also there and we got to talk about the ACA and Medicaid expansion. Several staffers I know went by and said hello. Two administration staffers were with me to talk about immigration reform. Then the president's secretary came to say that he was ready. We walked down the hall and he was standing by her desk. He greeted me, giving me a hug, and we went into the Oval Office.

And you know what? It really is a lot like the set from the *West Wing* television show!

The president sat in the chair and I sat on the couch across from him, just the two of us, and the photographer who stayed for a few minutes. I was just so stunned that it was just the two of us! I pulled out a tablet computer that I'd brought along so that I could show him our route and some pictures that we had taken so far so that he could get a flavor of the trip. Our projected route, he joked using a Bush-ism, "evidences some strategery!" I told him about the youthful community organizers in Camden and showed him shots of our "Raise your hands! Raise your voice!" mantra in action. He let me know and wanted me to tell everyone that he was committed to bipartisan, comprehensive immigration reform.

The meeting lasted about ten minutes, and as I was leaving he cautioned me not to wear myself out on this trip. I told him that since the whole thing was up to the Holy Spirit I figured we would be all right. I also returned the same caution to him—we needed his leadership, too, I said, and he must not to get too worn down in the process.

It was an amazing thing to meet with him, and a real grace for us, for our mission on behalf of social justice.

It's impossible to write an account of everything that happened in three weeks on the road but let me recall a few highlights.

In Charlotte, North Carolina, we took part in a business roundtable for immigration reform in which a local Realtor told us that the National Association of Hispanic Realtors did a study that indicated that three million of the estimated eleven million households with at least one member who is an undocumented person are poised to buy homes once their legal position is clarified and secure.

Then, as that meeting wrapped up, a Cuban-born couple and their daughter came up to me. They had driven more than five hundred miles from Lancaster, Pennsylvania, because they had seen me on television from Philadelphia and thought that I could be the answer to their terrible immigration situation. Their problems were complex, as is often the case in immigration cases. But this family was about to be torn apart because of our broken system and this man was so afraid now of the police because they had beaten him in the past and he feared that he would be deported and lose touch with his beloved family.

They were frantic and broke my heart. They wept, and I held them, and I cried. I tried to get them connected with resources in Charlotte so that they could get some help before I had to get on the bus to continue to South Carolina. I thought I was able to provide some assistance, and to calm their fears a bit. But it was agonizing. They thought I could be the answer to their prayers. The real answer, to their prayers and those of millions of others, was immigration reform. A new law. New policies. A new political dynamic for the common good. Episodes like those only pushed me to do more.

When we were close to Greenville, South Carolina, ahead of a stop at a local parish, we pulled into a mall parking lot for a pit stop. While we were there, a woman came running up to me. "Sister Simone! Hey, I'm so excited! I'm on my way to see you at St. Anthony's and here you are!" She gave me this huge hug, and I introduced her to the other sisters on the bus. She hugged all of us she was so excited. And frankly it was as much of a boost for us as it was for her. We were always surprised by the enthusiasm and recognition of our efforts, and it helped carry us across the continent.

When we got to Greenville, we were welcomed to St. Anthony Padua Church. We had a great briefing on the situation in South Carolina, and about halfway through the briefing the family from Pennsylvania came into the back of the church. They had followed us farther down the road!

At the end of the briefing, the family from Pennsylvania stood up and started to tell their story, speaking loudly in mixed Spanish and English to try to communicate. They began to say that immigration reform was for more than Mexican people, that it was for the Cuban people, too, for example. I got up and went to them to say of course immigration reform is for everyone. But they were in so much pain they could hardly hear anything that I said. So I held them, put my arms around them, and tried to comfort them. But that didn't work. So finally I just held them and I started to pray for them out loud in Spanish. I understand that the priest quickly came and stood with us, putting his hand on one of our shoulders. His action encouraged other people to come and stand with us and to put their hands on us. In the end we were all together in prayer for them and it eventually calmed them down a bit. It was tremendously powerful to be at the center of so much suffering and care!

In the end, the people of Greenville reached out to this family and seemed to make a good connection. The woman from the parking lot was at the center of trying to help. I made sure that they had a place for the night, legal representation, and someone to look after them at least for a few days. Finally, I made sure that the parish staff would help to connect them with some support back in Pennsylvania. Then, emotionally wrung out, we got on the bus again to head to Charleston for our evening friend-raiser.

In Charleston, after a great friend-raiser in the United Church of Christ's famous "circular church," we walked down to the slave market museum. The sin of our past is that so many came here as slaves. In this beautiful city, on this warm, dark evening, we committed ourselves to not repeating the mistakes of our past. We promised not to allow our nation to again create a permanent underclass of second-rank residents. We know that we must have a path to citizenship for all those who wish to follow it. This is required for us to be worthy of our ideals, and so that we do not repeat the sins of our past.

Two other stories from the bus stand out in my memory—twinned in motivation but so different in results.

The first took place on a blazing hot afternoon in San Antonio, Texas. We were holding an outdoor press event and rally to lobby for comprehensive immigration reform. Democratic congressman Pete Gallego, who had just come in from the airport after a trip, stepped to the podium with his prepared text. His eight-year-old son Nicholas was there and, oblivious of the huge crowd and all the cameras, ran up and threw his arms around his father's waist to welcome him home. The congressman was so touched that he put his papers down and spoke from the heart. He told us that his own attitude toward immigration reform was forever changed the first time he held Nicholas, right after the child was born. He told us that he knew in that moment that he would do whatever he could to protect his son. He would even give his life for his treasure. Any parent would, immigrant or native born. Tears welled up in our eyes as we listened and understood the deep truth that he was sharing as a parent, and the deep responsibility we shared for each other as citizens.

The second story came a few days later on the Pascua Yaqui reservation outside of Tucson, Arizona. After our briefing, the chairman of the Pascua Yaqui, Peter Yucupicio, told me of the horror of living on a reservation that was a pipeline for desperate immigrants trying to reach the United States. One day, he told me, he found the body of a woman curled up under a large desert bush where she had apparently sought shelter. When they turned her huddled body over, they found that she was cradling the body of her small child.

What immediately struck me was that this nameless woman had the same commitment to her child as Congressman Gallego had to his boy, and the same commitment parents everywhere share. The only difference is that her quest to protect her child, to provide a better life for her child, ended in the death of them both. This stark story is what comprehensive immigration reform is about and why we went back on the road.

I had always known that people without documents fear deportation, but I discovered this fear has many more nuances that I had ever imagined.

In Savannah, Georgia, for example, we met Ida, a seventeen-year-old who had finally received papers marking her Temporary Protected Status (TPS) and now had her learner's permit to drive. She was so terrified that her parents, who did not have papers, would get picked up by the police that she was doing all the family driving. She tells them not to go off with anyone after work and that she will come to pick them up. The roles are reversed in this family and the seventeen-year-old is the caregiver—of perfectly able-bodied parents limited only by the lack of a document.

At another stop, in Phoenix, Arizona, nineteen-year-old Jackie, who also had TPS papers, was raising her eleven-year-old twin siblings because both of their parents had been deported. Her fear? That she is not doing a good enough job raising them because she is so young.

At a Catholic Charities Center in Dallas we met young DREAM students—children of undocumented immigrants who qualified to apply for deferral of deportation under a 2012 order by President Obama to apply criteria of the still-unpassed DREAM Act, an acronym for Development, Relief, and Education for Alien Minors. It should be a law, but at least now children who came here as children have a chance to stay and fulfill the American dream. On this Saturday they came from near and far to apply for their own protected status. They came with their parents who were excited to be able to support their children in getting this protection from deportation. But in conversation with the teens, I found out that they felt a bit guilty that they could get protection but that their parents could not. This guilt made them ambivalent about even getting their own papers.

In Apopka, Florida, some of the DREAMers who came to the United States as young children greeted us with flags of the monarch butterfly. The monarch, they reminded us, migrates from the United States to Mexico and back each year. If the butterfly can travel without papers, they said, so should their families.

In El Paso, we met several "Social Security widows." These are senior citizens who had been married to U.S. citizens and were entitled to receive the Social Security widow's benefits—but if they were from Mexico and Central America, they had to spend a month each year in the United States to maintain that benefit. These elderly women were worrying about their capacity to continue to make the twenty-four-hour bus ride from Mexico City and parts even more distant from the United States. They worry about what they will do when they are not well enough to travel. This little known provision in the Social Security Code appears to be discriminatory against this particular group of especially vulnerable women. It opened our eyes to yet another form of suffering because of our broken immigration system.

In New Orleans, we met day laborers who had been imported to work in the city after the devastation of Hurricane Katrina. They are working every day to help rebuild the city. But they told terrible stories of having their wages stolen by employers and being harassed by immigration officials. They moved their families to New Orleans to help rebuild, and now the city and our nation are turning our backs on them.

In Nogales, Arizona, we were met by the mayor of the town on the Arizona side of the border. His counterpart from the Mexico side was supposed to be there to welcome us too, but he got stuck going through the checkpoint at the U.S. side of the border. No one knew what the holdup was, but he never made it to the event. The people of Nogales told us that this was common. Until

September 11, 2001, Nogales was basically one city with families stretched across the border. Now, with the wall that runs right through the middle of the combined city, it is almost impossible for families to get together.

The chairman of the Pascua Yaqui told us of a similar struggle. They have thirty thousand tribe members who hold Mexican passports and sixty thousand who hold U.S. passports. Every time they want to hold a tribal meeting, they have to deal with one of the nations to get visas and go back and forth across the border. The chairman said they are one people divided by two nations.

I wish I had answers for all these people. I wish I could help each and every one of them. We as individuals can of course do something, and every little bit is important. But we need to act together, as a nation, as a society, as a community, to fix our broken immigration system. And it is not just immigration reform; indeed, immigration is integral to who we are as a nation, to our identity, to our past—and to our future. This is not just an "issue." It is not just a single political clash, any more than health-care reform or the budget battles are games that we play during the silly season of campaign politics. Win some, lose some? No, this is about a process of becoming who we really are. Each issue, each battle, each stop on the bus, each story we heard, and each story I retell here, is part of our ongoing pilgrimage together. It is all of a piece. We are all one. We must move forward together, with our differences and disagreements. But we must air them, vote on them, not shut down the government, shut down dialogue, shut down the future.

I pray that we all might be inspired as we were on that last day of the bus tour, at the marina in San Francisco, when there was not a shred of fog on the bay and Angel Island stood out brightly against the dazzling sky. On that day we rallied one last time and shouted to the heavens: "Raise your hands! Raise your voice!"

Our nation needs that action, those voices. Our people need

it. Our families need it. Nothing is certain in politics, that's the one thing we know for sure. I also know that my spirituality calls me to walk willing with a broken heart—a brokenness that in the process of opening up releases hope for the many so that eventually justice for all our brothers and sisters may be realized. But until that day, we will stay in the struggle, walking in the dark and trusting that all things do work toward good.[47]

10

The Road Ahead

Faith and life experience have taught me that we are on a journey together. No one event will ever be *the* single solution. We must continue to work together, always, over and over again as necessary, opening ourselves to new experiences, to understanding new cultures and developments. The world is in many ways a global village—smaller than ever and yet more diverse than ever—and no one way is the "right" way forward.

In faith, we call this the journey of a "pilgrim people," always on the road, always moving ahead. Jesus sends us together into the world to bring good news to the poor, sight to the blind, freedom to captives. This news is brought in joy and, occasionally, on a bus. The key to living my faith is to know that listening deeply, in a contemplative stance, leads to trusting that we will find the next step, that it will be made visible, and that it will be important in some way that is much bigger than myself, my own journey.

Living my faith teaches me to know that we in creation are one body. All are important in this body even though we might have different functions. I sometimes joke that I might be the "stomach acid" in the body of Christ. But this acid is critical for metabolizing food and energizing life. It also might be that others are just as annoying—and critical—to the functioning of the entire body. No one is a mistake. No one is left out. This is why I am convinced by faith that we must strive for policies that include the 100 percent and involve the 100 percent in their formulation. It is a matter of being in right relationship with all of creation and in that way we will create a community that comes closer to being the "KIN-DOM" of God more than the "Kingdom" that we speak about.

Yet while I do this work because of my faith, I also recognize of course that in a pluralistic society there are many different perspectives. It is both unrealistic and wrong to insist that everyone hold my views, my faith. The place where we meet, in our differences, is in the founding documents of our democratic republic.

In the last half of the twentieth century, thankfully, our society began to engage in a serious process of trying to atone for the sin of slavery, and in doing so much emphasis was placed on promoting civil rights. An unintended consequence of this important movement was a heightened focus on individuals and individual exercise of the freedoms guaranteed in the Constitution. The civil rights movement came out of community, but the legal expression focused on individuals' capacity to exercise their freedoms. Some fearful Americans—largely white men who professed a conservative version of Christianity—felt threatened, as if there were not enough rights to go around. They sought to create their own "movement." This reaction in part fueled the rise of the tea party movement. It is almost as if a new group felt a need for its own Declaration of Independence in order to secure and protect its rightful place in our society.

But a democracy cannot survive if various groups and individuals only pull away in different directions. Such separation will not guarantee that *all* are allowed the opportunity for "life, liberty, and the pursuit of happiness." All people must be recognized for their inherent dignity and gifts regardless of the color of their skin, their religious beliefs, or their place of origin. And all these gifts need to be shared in order to build up the whole.

So I have begun to wonder if the new task of the first half of the twenty-first century should be a commitment to civil obligations as a balance to the focus on civil rights.

Civil obligations call each of us to participate out of a concern and commitment for the whole. Civil obligations call us to vote, to inform ourselves about the issues of the day, to engage in serious conversation about our nation's future and learn to listen to various perspectives. To live our civil obligations means that everyone needs to be involved and that there needs to be room for everyone to exercise this involvement. This is the other side of civil rights. We all need our civil rights so that we can all exercise our civil obligations.

This mandate to exercise our civil obligations means that we can't be bystanders who scoff at the process of politics while taking no responsibility. We all need to be involved. Civil obligations mean that we must hold our elected officials accountable for their actions, and we must advocate for those who are struggling to exercise their obligations. The 100 percent needs the efforts of all of us to create a true community.

It is an unpatriotic lie that we as a nation are based in individualism. The Constitution underscores the fact that we are rooted and raised in a communal society and that we each have a responsibility to build up the whole. The Preamble to the Constitution could not be any clearer: "We the People" are called to "form a more perfect Union." Absolute perfection is of course unattainable. Times change and needs arise, and we are required to adapt. And that requires an effort by all of us.

The central hypothesis in the experiment of democracy is the belief that people working together can govern themselves. Democracy demands that we as people solve our problems together. This is the antithesis of the concept of monarchy, a system that holds that one person (the king or queen) can solve our problems through royal edict. The framers of our Constitution knew that the only way that the fledgling democracy was going to function and survive was if there was a way for various constituencies to come together to solve problems. Only by meeting on common ground under shared principles can we govern ourselves and make decisions for the future.

Government becomes the way that democracies solve problems. If democracy is going to work, it can only be done by engaging in the hard tasks of problem solving. For us, today, an urgent problem is income inequality, the huge and growing gap, between the "haves" and the "have nots." Low-wage workers are struggling in poverty, and many of us are tempted to turn a blind eye to their plight as we focus on our own travails. But helping another means helping ourselves when viewed from the perspective of the common good. "Justice comes before charity," as many popes have said. We must always return to the pressing reality that our "more perfect union" is becoming less concerned about the general welfare. The general welfare requires paying a living wage and ensuring that all people can feed their families and be housed in dignity. We need to continue to strive to implement the Affordable Care Act and to make genuine, comprehensive immigration reform a reality. None of it will be perfect, but it will be a step forward in a new time for a new age.

What is essential is that we do this together in community. Our hope—dare I say our prayer?—must be that of Abraham Lincoln at Gettysburg 150 years ago: "That this nation, under God, shall have a new birth of freedom—and that government of the people, by the people, for the people, shall not perish from the earth." Government and politics is the way that we can turn those words into just laws and policies. It happens step-by-step.

It is my faith that keeps me on this path. On the good days, the contemplative life keeps me open to all of creation and gives me the energy to share this stance with others. On the more challenging days, the contemplative life sustains me through treasured uncertainty. I know at all times that the Spirit abides with all of us and will not leave us orphan. This is the promise that breaks hearts, releases hope, and, in the process, brings joy beyond understanding. This for me is living the Gospel in a turbulent world. This is the mission of NETWORK and the bus. So join us on the bus as we drive, and strive, for faith, family, and fairness. Join us in creating community so our democracy can survive. And join us in our fervent prayer:

"Come, Holy Spirit! Renew the face of the earth."

Poems for the Journey Ahead

ᕱ

Mysticism Matters

I yearn to practice
a mysticism that meets,
moves, mobilizes a piece of
the mundane world.
I hunger to use my gifts
of poetry and practicality,
of language and law to engage
part of the aching world.
My harness of Peter-ish
impetuosity matters not
at all, for I am hobbled
by blindness.
Please, use this moment
of light luminous
dark in time or no time
to reveal the next step.

Living Waters

Impetuous me favors the passionate tumult of Spring
river flooding. Sensuous me favors the indolent
caress of Summer river flowing. Reflective me
favors the penetrating seep of Autumn river trickling.
Even aloof shy me favors the chilled reserve of Winter
river freezing. But, all of me resists evaporation.

I resist the sucking pulling warm air wresting
me from known boundaries. I resist drifting unseen
to unknown parts. I resist the uncertainty of unformed
floating yearning rather to surround rocks, carve
new paths. I resist the ambiguous foggy drift.
But luckily, at times, I am yanked into air. There

beholding earth's
anguish: Weep!
Weeping, raining,
puddling . . . perhaps
the beginning of an
exuberant Spring.

Small Change

Dropped from the counter of globalization
in the midst of economic transactions,
these human coins, illegal tender
get swept up into the dust pan of
national identity and border security.
These small coins of labor fall through
the cracks of caring, ending up in
dank dark pens—smaller than pennies
in the global wealth, taken as too
small to matter, mere annoyances
or possible threat to a sovereign nation.
These small coins are tossed into cages
of fifty, sixty jumbled together
on the floor, in corners, along barred walls.
They do not fit into ATMs. They will not
be received for deposit in the world economy.
They are spare change tossed on the counter
of globalization—and forgotten.

Byzantium's Price

I.

The iconographer can work in words, actions
paints, enamels with equivalent results—
stark outlines of complex life reduced
to competing contrasts offering claret tunics,
scarlet cloaks, ebony eyes rimmed in silver
tears, terror. See them, this collection of raised
mortals, lifted above our heads to weep on us
argent insight, to light us to golden halo
hallowed truth.

II.

I am compelled to meticulously paint with steady
voice, steely nerves, aching heart my experience
of mid-Eastern life, of creature dailiness, human dread.
In the process, I pray these pictures penetrate
my neighbors' hearts. I am surprised, shocked,
grieving, I would say, about the price I am called
to pay. In the picture laden air, vivid before our eyes
the clear lined definition smooths, seals away
the rough edged complexity of actual life. Feather
frayed borders are finished, etched, sculpted into
precise single moments, sharpened to penetrate hearings'
hide. But listen close to the source of my lament—
I too lose the multi-layered impressionistic colors
of experience. Repeated telling distills my memories
to bold lines, primary colors—losing touch with
pulsing life.

III.

The last iconographic movement caresses these flat forms
and faces with liquid gold, wafer thin highlights
on legend lives leaving radiant marks of loss
in the crucible of telling—reducing details, impurities
in the white hot urgency of impasse. Faced with the
hunger of the hearer it is worth the rough edged loss
to grasp the chance, paying the price demanded by
this stark iconic gift to risk releasing hope into
the darkness.

Morum Conversio
(Daily Conversion of Life)

The challenge of stripping
wallpaper demands aggressive
questing for loose worn edges.
Ragged fingernails slip under
securing glue to liberate
a piece rewardingly wide or
frustratingly narrow—previously
applied in decorating fervor
removed in a new sensibility's disgust.
Did I ever like this gaudy hue?
Bits and pieces held too long need
a tougher treatment—spit,
water, determination. Pristine
walls reveal fifty-year-old notes:
"Wallpaper here." Ready for a
new design—a fresh start.

Jesus Wept

I.

Bold before me the businessman
laments Iraqi life—the impotence,
the waiting. Hunching forward he imparts
with strangled voice his secret view:
"I just want it over, one way or another,
we are dying slowly—let it be over soon."
A tear, unshed, pools in his eye,
he murmurs, "I have a child."

II.

The day my father cried for his daughter's
death, hides in the shadows of my memory.
At her grave, his shoulders hunched against
the pain, he held his breath and sealed
himself from the vivid world. One lone
tear escaped control sliding down the line
that marked his mourning. He shuddered
once and stilled again, adrift in grief.

III.

Be assured that fathers weep for children
lost. Fathers weep for dreams
destroyed. Fathers weep while the world
spins on.
O fathers, my fathers, stop
this madness, stop this march
to graves and grieving—
leave the tears unshed.

Compassion's Path

We walk a sandstorm of impotence,
isolated dread—the demons of our day.
We walk a sandstorm of half-truths,
lies of ochre, beige, tan, sepia confusion
pelted, buffeted by winds of war.
We walk a sandstorm of drifting elusive
truth, wandering ways and blind following.
We walk a sandstorm eroded by demanding
doubt, overwhelmed by the horror swirling
round invading lungs and lives.
We walk a sandstorm of promised grief,
aching temptation to hunker down, hide
until a more propitious time.
But in this time of alluring weakness,
in this time of fearful groaning, cold
blind logic, anger rising, remember
the clear eyed anchor of our resolve.
Remember the eyes of Mayada, Sara, Rita,
Assan, Abdullah, Makbulla and many more.
We may be blinded in the outward journey
but remember this inner core.
May the eyes of family, terrors of family
set fire to our impotence, stoke our resolve,
melt the cold stone of our hearts to yield
to tears. For like rain, tears shed settle
sand storms. Like rain, tears shed
clear the air. Like rain, tears shed
reveal the path. So let us weep.
Let us embody healing tears. Let us
be copious tears to settle our
country's storm.

Cultural Snag

The Mexican claret shawl drapes in informal
elegance across my Anglo shoulders. I lean into
the thin warmth, sheltering from the drizzle
breeze. The hugging textured center of this native
cotton cloth solidly claims my back, arms, wraps
round me, but, I confess, I detest the fringe.

I loathe the interfering fringe that catches on door
knobs, chair backs, rings, keys, a wide variety
of protruding parts of my jagged speeding world.
The pesky fringe jolts me in mid-certain stride
or dramatic gesture and snags the disquieting
wonder: Should this fluid disturbance to my warm
comfort be tolerated or snipped?

Coffee House Contemplation

Marvel at this convivial cup that quenches
a dual life—a jolt of froth and flavor,
foam and fragrance. Ah! Cappuccino!
Poised, waiting to be drunk, we see
the brown, the white, the blurring
line of demarcation.
But in the sacramental moment of
sipping—two are scorching one
then gone! Mmmm! Cappuccino!

Grief

A sudden onset of grief seeps
like humidity into all the crevices
of life. Like humidity, it hampers
lungs, constricts the heart, acts
as a barrier to rapid movement.
Humidity, sultry humidity, envelops
all of life, wilting the crisp edges
into human messiness. Humidity
like grief, eventually congeals,
coagulates, precipitates and weeps.
In clearing sorrow, life meanders
to the aching edges and waits
for promised dryer air, while treasuring
the all enveloping steamy incapacity
of grief.

Loaves and Fish

I always joked
that the miracle of loaves
and fish was: sharing.
The women always knew this.
But in this moment of need
and notoriety, I ache, tremble
almost weep at folks so
hungry, malnourished,
faced with spiritual famine
of epic proportions. My heart
aches with their need.
Apostle like, I whine:
"What are we among so many?"

The consistent 2000 year-old
ever-new response is this:
"Blessed and broken, you are
enough." I savor the blessed,
cower at the broken and
pray to be enough.

Ode to an Unmade Bed

The unmade bed served as mute testament
to the fullness of life exuberantly embraced—
a not looking back or worrying
about the unsquared corners.
Rumpled blankets grabbed
in the chill of midnight
tossed aside at dawn in the leap
for something new.

But this unmade bed served
as a haven in the darkness,
caressed evening weariness,
eased the sometimes ache of night.
Perhaps it goes unmade in tribute
to the chaos comforted,
to the ready welcome it offers
post toil, post tears.
Perhaps it goes unmade as a dream
catcher—so far beyond control
a tribute to faithful willingness
for something more.

Challenge to Be Church

Daunting undaunted autocrats agitate
my fluid world with righteous proclamations
stirring me up to equally righteous views—
claimed to protect myself, my different slice
of truth. But Incarnation—or is it Resurrection?
Pentecost?—all enliven me to know
we embody You, God, in all paradoxical life,
even the righteous defensive edges. I tremble
at Your call to love the autocrat—in them and me—
shedding the worry for my firm flimsy thoughts,
fragile self. Dare we risk a leap together,
plunging into darkness and being lost?
Or is it found?

Incarnation

Let gratitude be the beat of our heart,
pounding Baghdad rhythms, circulating
memories, meaning of the journey.

Let resolve flow in our veins,
fueled by Basra's destitution, risking
reflective action in a fifteen-second world.

Let compassion be our hands,
reaching to be with each other, all others
to touch, hold heal this fractured world.

Let wisdom be our feet,
bringing us to the crying need
to friends or foe to share this body's blood.

Let love be our eyes,
that we might see the beauty, see the dream
lurking in the shadows of despair and dread.

Let community be our body warmth,
radiating Arab energy to welcome in the foreign
stranger—even the ones who wage this war.

Let us remember on drear distant days,
we are a promised Christmas joy
we live as one this fragile gifted life—for

We are the Body of God!

ACKNOWLEDGMENTS

R eader, please know that until this moment I have never understood the depth of gratitude that tries to get expressed in a few short sentences of acknowledgment. Please think of what you are most grateful for and read my words with that sentiment.

I am profoundly grateful to David Gibson for his collaboration in making this book happen. Without David's determination and willingness to pursue this story, this book would not be in print. His humor, faith, and willingness to adventure made this possible.

And for Roger Freet, our editor at HarperOne, I am grateful that his imagination realized that David and I might fit well together in this project. While I call this match "an arranged marriage," Roger's matchmaking and mentoring made this book a reality.

My gratitude is overflowing for all of my sisters around the country whom I have met and those I have not. Our "sister-hood" is a treasured connection that has allowed us to lift up our profound care for those who are most left out of our society. Our vocation is a sacred gift in these turbulent times and I delight that we get to live this mission together.

Finally, this book would not exist without the hundreds of people I've met and stories that I have heard. Each person and community has enriched my life and hopefully made me a better person. So many of you have broken my heart and given me hope. So many have challenged me to grow and think more deeply about the issues of our times. So many have nurtured me and shown me God alive in our world. To all of you in this vibrant body of creation: THANK YOU!

NOTES

1. The term "women religious" refers to all women who take vows of poverty, chastity, and obedience in a community, such as the Franciscans, Dominicans, or one of the hundreds of other lesser known orders. "Nuns," properly speaking, are cloistered women who take the habit and are devoted to a life of prayer, and work within the walls of a monastery. "Sisters" like myself often live in community, but not always, and we work out in the world—traditionally by helping the sick and the poor, or as teachers—but more recently as hospital executives and lawyers, pursuing the corporal works of mercy in boardrooms and courts. The difference between sisters and nuns is generally described as the difference between an "active" and "contemplative" religious life, but there is really no bright line between them. Many contemplative nuns also work outside the convent for a few hours a day or more, and we active sisters are grounded in a deeply contemplative prayer life. So the terms are often interchangeable, and though we "Nuns on the Bus" are really sisters, not nuns, who could pass up such a catchy slogan?
2. See *Vatican News* from November 29, 2013, www.news.va/en/news/meeting -with-the-superiors-general-the-pope-announ.
3. Sister Margaret Slachta, *From the Desert to the Center of Life*, private publication of the Sisters of Social Service, circa 1928: 23.

4. See Exodus 16.

5. Quoted in Paul Vitello, "Anita Caspary, Nun Who Led Breakaway from Church, Dies at 95," *New York Times*, October 18, 2011.

6. For information on Pope Benedict's encyclical and the response to it, see http://ncronline.org/blogs/essays-theology/popes-social-encyclical.

7. Minutes of the founding meeting of the Sisters of Social Service, Budapest, Hungary, May 12, 1923.

8. Sister Margaret Slachta, *From the Desert to the Center of Life*, private publication of the Sisters of Social Service, circa 1928, p. 20.

9. See www.sistersofsocialservice.com/history.cfm for historical information on the Sisters of Social Service.

10. From Walter Brueggemann's *The Prophetic Imagination*, 2nd ed. (Minneapolis, MN: Fortress Press, 2001): 57.

11. The information on Dom Willigis Jäger is from http://en.wikipedia.org/wiki/Willigis_J%C3%A4ger.

12. Reverend Hawk died in 2012. See more at www.desertrenewal.org/rrc/programs/pathless_path.html.

13. To learn more about the Jericho organization, see www.jerichoca.org/about.htm.

14. See www.catholicnews.com/data/stories/cns/1100290.htm and www.sistersofmercy.org/index.php?option=com_content&task=view&id=170&Itemid=205.

15. See www.catholicnews.com/data/stories/cns/1104044.htm.

16. See www.nytimes.com/2012/06/09/us/suicides-eclipse-war-deaths-for-us-troops.html and http://dish.andrewsullivan.com/2013/03/29/the-cost-of-the-iraq-afghanistan-wars/.

17. For basic background information on the PPACA debate, see http://en.wikipedia.org/wiki/Patient_Protection_and_Affordable_Care_Act#Health_care_debate.2C_2008.E2.80.932010.

18. General background material on the Stupak Amendment is from http://en.wikipedia.org/wiki/Stupak%E2%80%93Pitts_Amendment.

19. Thomas Merton, *Zen and the Birds of Appetite* (New Directions Press: New York, 196): 56.

20. The Democrats for Life Caucus is a loose association of Democrats that support alternatives to abortion. Those who were identified with the caucus and lost in the 2010 election include: Rep. John Boccieri (D-Ohio); Rep. Steve Driehaus (D-Ohio); Rep. Mary Jo Kilroy (D-Ohio); Rep. Kathy Dahlkemper (D-Pa.); Rep. Patrick Murphy (D-Pa.); Rep. Ciro Rodriguez (D-Texas); Rep. Ann Kirkpatrick (D-Ariz.); Rep. Phil Hare (D-Ill.); Rep. Charlie Wilson (D-Ohio); Rep. Chris Carney (D-Pa.); and Rep. Baron Hill (D-Ind.).

21. Richard Wilkinson and Kate Pickett, *The Spirit Level* (New York: Blooms-
    bury Press, 2009).
22. According to a Census Bureau report, households in the lowest quin-
    tile had incomes of $20,262 or less in 2011. See www.census.gov/
    prod/2012pubs/p60-243.pdf.
23. Figure 3, The real value of the minimum wage, actual vs. hypothetical
    at various growth rates. Economic Policy Institute, www.epi.org/blog/
    putting-9-minimum-wage-context.
24. Sources for Bishop Blaire's testimony and statistics include http://dish
    .andrewsullivan.com/2013/06/25/maximizing-the-minimum-wage/ and
    www.uscatholic.org/articles/201306/economics-inequality-why-wealth
    -gap-bad-everyone—27421.
25. Pope Francis's quotes are included in the Catholic News Service re-
    port for April 4, 2013, found at www.catholicnews.com/data/stories/
    cns/1301525.htm.
26. Pope Francis's landmark interview was conducted by Antonio Spadaro
    of *La Civiltà Cattolica* and was published worldwide in a number of Jesuit
    publications.
27. See http://attualita.vatican.va/sala-stampa/bollettino/2013/04/15/
    news/30807.htm.
28. From an unofficial transcript of the meeting report of meeting found at
    http://ncronline.org/blogs/distinctly-catholic/pope-francis-pelagians
    -gnostics-and-cdf.
29. See http://sojo.net/blogs/2012/08/13/nuns-reject-vatican-takeover-seek
    -dialogue-differences for background here.
30. See www.nytimes.com/2012/06/06/us/us-nuns-bus-tour-to-spotlight
    -social-issues.html.
31. My following remarks can be heard on the YouTube video at www.youtube
    .com/watch?v=Xd7W4rN-aXs.
32. For the story of the bus kickoff (and Steve King's staff's nonappearance)
    here and following, see http://ncronline.org/news/politics/nuns-bus
    -kicks-nationwide-tour-iowa.
33. From http://thegazette.com/2012/06/22/nuns-shared-sacrifice-pitch
    -rings-true/.
34. See www.youtube.com/watch?v=SZ1ff3NYsQA and www.dailykos
    .com/story/2012/06/20/1101550/-Nuns-on-the-Bus-in-Janesville-WI
    -protesting-Paul-Ryan-s-budget#.
35. See http://en.wikipedia.org/wiki/Overpass_Light_Brigade.
36. See www.freerepublic.com/focus/f-news/2069428/posts, http://
    ncronline.org/blogs/ncr-today/dolans-gop-prayer-causes-stir, and

http://anunslife.org/blog/nun-talk/sister-catherine-pinkerton
-prayer-dnc.

37. For background, see http://archives.religionnews.com/politics/election/
cardinal-dolans-gop-convention-blessing-prompts-debate.

38. Other sources for the events surrounding the convention include: http://
content.usatoday.com/communities/Religion/post/2012/08/republican
-national-convention-democrat-cardinal-dolan/1#.UdqWWlOhvVo;
www.networklobby.org/news-media/press-release-sister-simone
-campbell-speak-democratic-national-convention; and http://archives
.religionnews.com/politics/election/cardinal-dolan-will-bless-the
-democratic-convention-nuns-too.

39. See www.sistersofsocialservice.com/MargaretSlachta.cfm.

40. From http://thegrio.com/2012/09/06/democratic-convention-beats
-football-in-ratings/.

41. View the speech at www.youtube.com/watch?v=ASmM2YHxsfs.

42. Michael Hoefer, Nancy Rytina, and Bryan Baker, "Estimates of the Un-
authorized Immigrant Population Residing in the United States: January
2011," *Population Estimates* (2012): www.dhs.gov/sites/default/files/publi-
cations/ois_ill_pe_2011.pdf.

43. "Annual Report of Immigrant Visas in the Family-sponsored and
Employment-based preferences Registered at the National Visa Center as
of November 1, 2013," www.travel.state.gov/pdf/WaitingListItem.pdf.

44. Julianne Hing, "Are Immigrants Flooding the Military for U.S. Citizenship?" *Colorlines* (2011): http://colorlines.com/archives/2011/07/are
_immigrants_flooding_the_military_for_us_citizenship.html.

45. "The Fallacy of 'Enforcement First,'" (2013): www.immigrationpolicy
.org/just-facts/fallacy-enforcement-first.

46. "The Cost of Doing Nothing," (2013): www.immigrationpolicy.org/
just-facts/cost-doing-nothing.

47. Some sites information on the immigration bus tour was drawn from
include: www.religionnews.com/2013/07/25/nuns-on-the-bus
-push-congress-to-pass-immigration-reform/; www.religionnews
.com/2013/05/01/nuns-on-the-bus-will-hit-the-road-for-immigration
-reform/; www.religionnews.com/2013/05/29/nuns-on-the-bus-kick
-off-immigration-tour/.